# Bin the bucket and spade

# Bin the bucket and spade

Unusual
family holidays
in the usual
destinations

**Paul Jenner
and Christine Smith**

Editor: Roni Jay

WHiTe
LaDDEr
PRESS

new tricks for old dogs

Published by White Ladder Press Ltd

Great Ambrook, Near Ipplepen, Devon TQ12 5UL

01803 813343

**www.whiteladderpress.com**

First published in Great Britain in 2007

10 9 8 7 6 5 4 3 2 1

ISBN 978 1 905410 18 7

British Library Cataloguing in Publication Data

A CIP record for this book can be obtained from the British Library.

Designed and typeset by Julie Martin Ltd
Cover design by Julie Martin Ltd
Cover photograph Jonathon Bosley
Printed and bound by TJ International Ltd, Padstow, Cornwall
Cover printed by St Austell Printing Company
Printed on totally chlorine-free paper
The paper used for the text pages of this book is FSC certified.
FSC (The Forest Stewardship Council) is an international
network to promote responsible management of the world's forests.

**FSC**
Mixed Sources
Product group from well-managed
forests and other controlled sources

Cert no. SGS-COC-2482
www.fsc.org
© 1996 Forest Stewardship Council

White Ladder books are distributed in the UK by Virgin Books

**White Ladder Press**
**Great Ambrook, Near Ipplepen, Devon TQ12 5UL**
**01803 813343**
**www.whiteladderpress.com**

# Acknowledgements

We would like to thank all those who took part in our survey and especially the staff and children of Horsell Church of England Junior School in Surrey.

# Contents

# Holiday Checklist

## KEY

| | | | |
|---|---|---|---|
| T = Toddlers | Y = Yes | Sp = Spring | 1 = Budget |
| P = Pre-Teens | X = No | S = Summer | 2 = Medium |
| Ad = Adolescents | | A = Autumn | 3 = Expensive |
| | All = Various | W = Winter | 4 = Various |

| Holiday | Best For | Active | When | Cost |
|---|---|---|---|---|
| No.1: The Water Wow Crowd | P Ad | All | All | 3 |
| No. 2: The Approval Of Seals | P Ad | X | SA | 1–2 |
| No. 3: The Bird Buzz | P Ad | All | All | 1–2 |
| No. 4: The Magic Of Mammals | P Ad | All | All | All |
| No. 5: Up Close And Personal | T P Ad | All | All | All |
| No. 6: Barcelona | P Ad | X | Sp S A | All |
| No. 7: Athens | P Ad | X | Sp S A | All |
| No. 8: Rome | P Ad | X | Sp S A | All |
| No. 9: New York | P Ad | X | All | 2–3 |
| No.10: Paris | P Ad | X | Sp S A | 2–3 |
| No.11: London | P Ad | X | Sp S A | All |
| No. 12: In The Swim | P Ad | Y | S | All |
| No. 13: Snorkelling | P Ad | Y | S | All |
| No. 14: Diving | Ad | Y | S | 2–3 |
| No. 15: Surfing | Ad | Y | All | All |
| No. 16: Dinghy Sailing and Windsurfing | P Ad | Y | S | 2–3 |
| No. 17: Sea Kayaking | T P Ad | Y | S | 2–3 |
| No. 18: Beach Riding | P Ad | Y | All | 3 |
| No. 19: Cruising | T P Ad | All | S | 3 |
| No. 20: Children's Clubs | T P Ad | Y | S W | 2 |

| Holiday | Best For | Active | When | Cost |
|---|---|---|---|---|
| No. 21: Summer Camps | P Ad | Y | S | 2–3 |
| No. 22: Summer Schools | P Ad | All | S | 2–3 |
| No. 23: Riding | P Ad | Y | All | 2–3 |
| No. 24: Hiking | P Ad | Y | All | All |
| No. 25: Orienteering | P Ad | Y | All | All |
| No. 26: Cycling And Mountain Biking | P Ad | Y | All | All |
| No. 27: Climbing | P Ad | Y | All | All |
| No. 28: Ghost Hunting | Ad | Y | All | All |
| No. 29: White Water Rafting | Ad | Y | S | 2–3 |
| No. 30: Canyoning – Nature's Waterpark | Ad | Y | S | 2–3 |
| No. 31: Paddling Your Own Canoe | P Ad | Y | S | All |
| No. 32: Messing About In Boats | T P Ad | Y | S | 2–3 |
| No. 33: On The Cut | T P Ad | All | S | 1–2 |
| No. 34: Multi-Sports | P Ad | Y | S | 2–3 |
| No. 35: Fact And Fiction | P Ad | X | All | All |
| No. 36: Music And Arts Festivals | T P Ad | X | S | All |
| No. 37: Learn The Language | T P Ad | X | All | All |
| No. 38: Ask The Experts | P Ad | X | S | All |
| No. 39: Arty-Crafty Holidays | P Ad | X | S | All |
| No. 40: Teach Yourself Holidays | T P Ad | X | All | All |
| No. 41: Voyages Of Discovery | T P Ad | X | S | 3 |
| No. 42: It's Carnival Time | T P Ad | X | All | All |
| No. 43: The Frisson Of Fireworks | T P Ad | X | All | All |
| No. 44: VAT – Value Added Travel | T P Ad | X | All | All |
| No. 45: Europa-Park | T P Ad | X | S W | 2–3 |
| No. 46: Gardaland | T P Ad | X | S | 2–3 |
| No. 47: Tivoli Gardems | T P Ad | X | S | 2–3 |
| No. 48: Puy Du Fou | T P Ad | X | S | 2–3 |
| No. 49: Futuroscope | T P Ad | X | S | 2–3 |
| No. 50: Warner Bros. Movie World | T P Ad | X | Sp S A | 2–3 |
| No. 51: Phantasialand | T P Ad | X | S W | 2–3 |
| No. 52: Specialist Operators | T P Ad | All | S | 2 |

| Holiday | Best For | Active | When | Cost |
|---|---|---|---|---|
| No. 53: Friends Abroad | T P Ad | X | All | 1 |
| No. 54: Home Swapping | T P Ad | X | All | 1 |
| No. 55: Diving And Snorkelling* | Ad | Y | S | 2–3 |
| No. 56: Skiing* | P Ad | Y | W | 2–3 |
| No. 57: Animal Assisted Therapy* | P Ad | Y | All | 2–3 |
| No. 58: Sailing* | Ad | Y | S | All |
| No. 59: Downhill Skiing | P Ad | Y | W | 2–3 |
| No. 60: Snowboarding | P Ad | Y | W | 2–3 |
| No. 61: Cross-Country Skiing | P Ad | Y | W | All |
| No. 62: Ski Touring | Ad | Y | W | 2–3 |
| No. 63: Dog Mushing | T P Ad | Y | W | 3 |
| No. 64: Looking For The *Real* Father Christmas | T P Ad | X | W | All |
| No. 65: Christmas On The Beach | T P Ad | X | W | 2–3 |
| No.66: Hogmanay | Ad | X | W | 4 |

**\* For disabled children**

# Introduction

What makes a really good family holiday? We thought we knew. After all, we used to be children ourselves, once. And we've taken children and grandchildren many times. But, just to be sure, and with the help of Horsell Church Of England Junior School in Surrey, we checked with over 150 children, of whom just over half were girls. Some of the answers to our questionnaire surprised us.

## Responses to the questionnaire

### Who decides where to go?

A whopping 87% of children surveyed said their parents consulted them about where to go on holiday. And almost as many (81%) said their parents took notice of their views. Well, that's what the kids believe, anyway.

### If you were allowed to choose anywhere, where would you go?

We were rather impressed by the adventurous and outward looking answers to this question.

The figures are good for the USA which was by far the most popular destination, chosen by more than a quarter of children. They're good for Australia, a surprising second place selected by 14%. And they seem to guarantee the continuing popularity of Spain which was in third place at 10%. Interestingly, the next two places were taken by the Caribbean and Africa, no doubt reflecting a multicultural Britain.

The figures aren't very encouraging for the UK tourism industry. Only two and a half per cent of children said that was *the* place they wanted to take a holiday. And, on this showing, Asia needs to do a lot more to raise its profile with children.

These were the favourite destinations:

| | Percentage of youngsters choosing |
|---|---|
| America | 27 |
| Australia | 14 |
| Spain | 10 |
| Caribbean | 9 |
| Africa | 8 |
| Italy | 6 |
| New Zealand | 4 |
| France | 4 |

Other destinations specifically mentioned included Canada, Greenland, Antarctica, Dubai, Mexico, Papua New Guinea, Bora Bora, Hong Kong, China and Japan.

## What sort of things do you like doing on holiday?

Pay attention, parents. The vast majority of children surveyed (just over 70%) said they liked going to the beach and swimming. And a further 10% specifically mentioned sunbathing. So beach holidays are extremely important to youngsters. Now, although we've called this book *Bin The Bucket And Spade*, that certainly doesn't mean we've neglected beach holidays. It simply means we've found beach ideas that are a bit more exciting than the usual. Because one thing for sure is that youngsters do like having things to do. Around a quarter of youngsters mentioned specific activities in addition to swimming.

Interestingly, sightseeing and theme parks scored the same, being mentioned by around nine per cent of children.

Only three children – all girls, as it happens – specifically mentioned skiing. But that probably reflects the fact that very few actually had any experience of winter sports. We think the snow is the winter equivalent of the beach – a natural for families and it's the subject of Chapter 14.

There were some predictable differences between girls and boys. Four times as many girls as boys mentioned shopping as an agreeable holiday activity and three times as many girls as boys mentioned sunbathing. Girls were slightly less interested in physical activities and slightly more interested in food and going out at night. Six girls said they liked to meet people and make friends on holiday whereas no boys mentioned that concept at all.

**Describe your best and worst holidays**

When we asked children to describe their best and worst holidays we got a slightly different picture. It seems the things that really make or break a holiday are specific incidents that either leave a pleasant memory or a bad memory.

In one case it was a game of mini-golf that made the holiday, in another it was seeing a turtle, in another driving a go-kart, in another a mountain bike and in another riding a camel.

Holidays were spoiled by things like mould on the wall, people not being friendly, delay at the airport and bad food.

But there were some very clear general rules.

The recipe for a good holiday is hot, sunny weather (but not too hot), being with friends and family and having *lots to do* especially theme parks and swimming. Eleven children said that having a private swimming pool was the most important ingredient in their best holiday and six nominated swimming with dolphins while one mentioned a sting ray.

Here, in order of importance, are the things children mentioned the most:

- Swimming
- Good weather
- Lots to do
- Friends and family
- Theme parks

The recipe for a bad holiday is bad weather, an injury or illness, creepy crawlies and annoying people, including relatives.

**Would you like to go on holiday without your parents?**

Brace yourselves, parents. According to our survey, your children would probably prefer to go on holiday without you. That, anyway, is what 57% of children said. Of course, that's not necessarily bad news. Because if they want to go on holiday without you, you can go on holiday without them. Without feeling any guilt. It doesn't mean they don't love you. It just means they think they'll have a better time in the company of youngsters their own age. There was very little difference between the sexes on this one.

## How much spending money are you given on holiday?

Answers to this question varied considerably and, quite frankly, we decided to exclude some of the more extravagant ones. We couldn't believe, for example, that anybody would be given £500 to spend. After making those allowances, the average holiday spending money worked out at just over £18.

A quarter of boys and a sixth of girls were given no spending money at all, suggesting either that girls are better at wheedling money out of parents and relatives or are simply considered more responsible. On the other hand, when boys are given spending money they seem to get more than girls. According to our survey, those boys who were given money received an average of £27 as against £20 for girls. So it seems the inequality of the sexes in financial matters has already begun.

We also asked children if they were allowed to spend their holiday money as they liked. Again there was a difference between boys and girls. Three-quarters of girls said they were free to spend their money as they chose but just under two-thirds of boys said the same. It seems to confirm the notion that boys are considered to be less responsible.

## Travel Tips For Kids

### Transport

Most children find flying a pretty exciting experience but after a couple of hours sitting in a seat even the most enthusiastic can find things tedious. Some children are happy reading a book but others need entertaining. Pocket sized games are a good idea – chess, draughts. Check with the cabin crew before using electronic devices. A little preparation beforehand can help. For example, you could trace the flight path on a map and watch out for identifiable features below, at least if you have clear weather.

Even with today's pressurised cabins there are pressure differences which can cause pain to tiny ears. See a doctor about any ear infection and try to get it cleared up before you fly. Nursing a baby can help relieve their ear pain; older children can suck sweets.

The biggest environmental impact of your holiday will be the flight. If you want to know exactly how much damage you're doing and what you can do to help put it right, see **www.climatecare.org** Tel: 01865 207 000. There's an Air Travel Calculator on the website so that you can contribute the appropriate amount to reforestation and other schemes to combat global warming.

Motion sickness always has a psychological aspect. Try to distract susceptible children who, by focussing on their feelings may otherwise 'talk themselves' into feeling ill.

## Sightseeing

When it isn't possible to be doing the kinds of things children like it's a good idea to have a few tricks up your sleeve. Younger children are easily motivated by tales of things like hidden treasure. The idea is simple and can be adapted as circumstances dictate. You announce that you've heard of a princess/pirate/soldier/explorer or whoever who apparently hid some treasure in the area. You prepare a treasure map and clues (suitably aged with a little dirt) and hide the first clue where it's certain to be found. Any children who are complaining about sightseeing generally stop moaning when clues mysteriously turn up at all the sites you want to see.

## Food

Foreign food is much less of a problem than it once was simply because all children nowadays eat 'foreign' food as a matter of course. Things like spaghetti, lasagne, pizza, ratatouille and curry are mainstays of the 'British' diet. On the other hand, dishes such as sauerkraut, snails and squid don't always go down too well.

Don't panic if your children refuse to eat very much. One or two weeks of poor diet aren't really very significant. If you're anticipating problems then it might be a good idea to book some form of self-catering accommodation. That way you can prepare the kinds of meals the kids have at home.

## Health

Quite a lot of kids (and adults, too) get upset stomachs on holiday. It doesn't mean the food is dirty. There are bacteria everywhere and on holiday they're simply different bacteria to the ones everybody is used to at home. So it's a good idea to be prepared with something for holiday diarrhoea.

## Prices

To save you having to look up exchange rates and do arithmetic we've converted all foreign prices to pounds at the rates prevailing at the beginning of 2007. For that reason they should only be taken as a rough guide.

# Chapter 1

# The Call Of The Wildlife

**Unusual family holidays in this chapter: watching whales, dolphins, seals, manatees, bald eagles, burrowing owls, dormice, bats, and much more.**

Children love animals. It's just a fact of life. So we're starting off with holidays that involve animals because they're bound to be a success. More than that, seeing wild animals and being able to interact in some way is good for children's development and mental health. And it does adults a power of good, too, to reconnect with nature. Sadly, it's not as easy to see wild animals as it once was, especially not in Europe. But here we tell you some of the best places and best operators.

You can also find operators specialising in wildlife holidays at **www.travel-quest.co.uk**

## Unusual Family Holiday No. 1: The Water Wow Crowd

Ask children to write down the animals they'd most like to see and be with – the ones that most make them say Wow! – and dolphins will come high on most lists. And adults feel the same way. Is it simply that dolphins wear a permanent smile? Or is it that we all sense that dolphins have some kind of special power? Anybody interested should read Rachel Smolker's wonderful book *To Touch A Wild Dolphin*.

We've seen wild dolphins several times from the deck of our yacht but, unfortunately, actually swimming with wild dolphins remains an ambition still to be fulfilled. On one occasion the dolphins put on a spectacular show in the bow wave and made deliberate eye contact. It's something we'll never forget.

Let's start with the UK. Not many people realise that nearly a third of the world's species of whales, dolphins and porpoises have been reported in Hebridean waters including, on occasion, the blue whale. The Isle of Mull is to whale and dolphin spotting what Hollywood is to film star sightings – the celebrities are often there but only show themselves when *they* want to. Another excellent UK Wow Factor destination is Cardigan Bay, where operators of rigid inflatables claim a 95 per cent success rate for dolphins and a 40 per cent chance of sighting minke, fin or sei whales.

Off the coast of West Cork in summer (**www.whalewatchwestcork.com** Tel: 00 353 861 200 027) there's a good chance of minke, fin and even humpback whales but even if you don't see them you'll almost certainly see short beaked common dolphins, whose numbers have been on the increase in the area.

Heading south, one of the surest, easiest and most accessible places to see dolphins and whales is the Straits of Gibraltar, where some 50 resident dolphins are joined each summer by several hundred common, bottlenose and striped companions. The skippers who specialise in this can virtually guarantee an encounter. You can sometimes even see orcas competing with the blue fin tuna fishermen for their catch. You can get a boat from Gibraltar itself or nearby Spanish resorts on the Costa del Sol and the Costa de la Luz. The secret of a profoundly moving experience is a small boat with no more than a dozen people – avoid the big ones.

Slightly further afield, 28 species of dolphins and whales reside in or migrate through the waters south-west of La Gomera in the Canary Islands. The season is March to November but *excluding* June and the first half of July. You can make arrangements when you get there or book an inclusive package – take a look at the internet travel agency **www.responsibletravel.com** which offers a one week package featuring half-day excursions in a traditional fishing boat. La Gomera is one of the wildest of the Canary group and when you've finished at sea you might like to explore the Garajonay National Park, for which UNESCO has made the island a World Heritage Site.

If you're looking for more serious involvement, then your family may enjoy the sort of trips organised by The Whale and Dolphin Conservation Society **www.wdcs.org**. There's a specialist six day package with guided daily trips based at Tarifa, Spain, while in the Ligurian Sea (between Italy, France and Corsica) there's the chance to live aboard for a week, helping scientists monitor various animals including the 20m long, 70 ton fin whales.

Right out in the Atlantic, the Whale Watch Azores Project involves boat trips of up to six days and is suitable for adults and teenagers who want to get involved in photo-identification and tracking **www. whalewatchazores.com** Tel:01295 267652.

Possibly the greatest place to see whales in the whole world is California, where commercial whale watching began in 1955 with Chuch Chamberlin's $1 boat trips. Winter is the time for grey whales and summer for blue whales, the biggest creatures that have ever lived on Earth, when several hundred gather in the Santa Barbara Channel. Further up the coast at Monterey you may also see porpoises, dolphins, up to seven species of whales, sea lions and sea otters. Take a look at the American Cetacean Society site **www.acsonline.org** for general information and try **www.montereybaywhalewatch.com** and **www.sanctuarycruises.com** for trips. You can combine your California whale watching with visits to Yosemite (see **www.nps.gov/yose** and **www.yosemitepark.com**) for black bears, mule deer and bighorn sheep, while in the Mojave desert (**www.nps.gov/moja**) you might see mountain lion.

---

### Campaign Against Whaling

We debated whether or not to include Iceland in this book, now that its government has decided to resume the killing of whales. If you make the three hour flight from Heathrow you'll stand a high chance of seeing blue whales off Snaefellsnes (**www.arctic-experience.co.uk** Tel: 01737 214 214) and give whales an economic value *alive*. On the other hand, you could boycott Iceland in favour of a country that doesn't hunt whales. Whichever you decide, be sure to let the tourist office know how much you disapprove of whaling by sending an e-mail to **info@ice-tourist.is**. You might also like to join Greenpeace. (**www.greenpeace.org.uk**).

---

### Children And Boats

For young children a boat trip of two or three hours will probably be enough. Whole day and multi-day trips are more suitable for older children. Obviously, a lot depends on the boat and the weather. Inevitably, there will be periods when there's nothing much to see, except, well, sea. So a little preparation is a good idea.

Make sure the kids can identify the various animals they're likely to spot and know a little about them. The BBC's *Deep Blue*, available on DVD, is a great place to start. Encourage them to make their own sketches and notes and take photographs, all of which can be combined in a scrapbook. Some of the longer trips include talks and lectures as well as the chance to take part in research projects.

On a more practical level, make sure there's plenty of food and drink and ask the organisers to advise on suitable clothing. If seasickness threatens, the best treatment is to get face down on a bunk, lying fore and aft (that's to say, along the boat not across it). When no bunk is available it's usually best to keep out in the open air (but warm) where the movement of the boat is less noticeable. There are various remedies available from chemists but we recommend the traditional fresh ginger chewed very slowly.

## FURTHER INFORMATION

Good places to start are **www.whaleguide.com** and **www.whale watchingtours.com** which give links to a variety of tour operators. The Whale and Dolphin Conservation Society website (**www.wdcs.org** Tel: 0870 870 5001) has news and a holiday section called 'Into The Blue' offering a wide range of marine mammal encounters. For a Scottish slant look up **www.whaledolphintrust.co.uk** or **www.seescotlanddifferently.co.uk**. For important news of what's going on in the battle to protect the world's seas click on **www.oceanalliance.org** or **http://oceans.greenpeace.org** or **www.panda.org** (World Wildlife Fund).

### Some specialist operators

**www.naturetrek.co.uk** Tel: 01962 733 051

**www.responsibletravel.com** Tel: 01273 600 030

**www.wdcs.org** Tel: 0870 8705 0001

**www.montereywhalewatching.com** Tel: 800 2002203 (within the USA)

**www.dolphinclick.de** Tel: 0034 92 280 5717

**www.azoreswhales.com** Tel:00 351 29 662 8522

**www.discoveryinitiatives.com** Tel: 01285 643 333

### Some questions to ask

✓ What is the minimum age?

✓ How certain are sightings?

✓ What sort of boat are you operating?

✓ Is there cover for bad weather?

✓ How many passengers on the boat?

✓ Will there be food/drink?

✓ Are there toilets?

✓ Is there anybody to explain what we see?

## Why is this good for families?

Regardless of age or sex, everybody will be thrilled.

## Pros

- An almost mystical experience that will be the highlight of any holiday.
- Educational.
- Something impressive to write about in any 'What I did on my holidays' essay.

## Cons

- Possibly cold and wet.
- Seasickness.

## Where to go

Scotland, Wales, Ireland, Straits of Gibraltar, Canary Islands, Azores, Ligurian Sea, California.

## When

Mostly summer, but winter for grey whales off California.

## Price Guide

A boat trip of around two to three hours should cost from around £15, a short live aboard trip from around £250 and a full holiday package up to £1,500.

# Unusual Family Holiday No. 2: The Approval Of Seals

To many of us, seals may sound like rather exotic creatures that only live on remote islands towards the Poles. But in fact, many of the 80,000 north-east Atlantic population of grey seals – about half the world's total – are to be found around the shores of Britain and

Ireland. These are impressive animals. A full grown adult male will weigh up to 300kg and eat about 6kg of fish a day – which is why they've been persecuted. Even the smaller common seals can weigh up to 130kg.

Whichever the type, seals are generally more reliable than whales and dolphins *during the breeding season*. If a trip organiser claims you'll see seals – you almost certainly will. You'll probably see the pups as well – newborn grey seals have a crumpled, white protective coat for about two or three weeks while common seal pups normally lose their white, woolly coat just before birth.

Grey seals favour rocky coastlines, common seals prefer sandbanks. Best areas in the UK are Scotland, Northumberland (including up to 4,000 grey seals on the Farne Islands), Seal Island in the Wash (the largest colony of common seals in Europe), Blakeney Point in Norfolk, the Pembrokeshire island of Ramsey and Cardigan Bay (Wales). As regards the Mediterranean, the Monk seal is, sadly, one of the world's most endangered animals and trips to its few remaining breeding places are inadvisable (but see *Up Close And Personal*, below). If you want to see the world's largest mainland colony of the amazing giant northern elephant seals (and who wouldn't?) then it's in California. Just 50 miles or so south of San Francisco at Point Piedras Blancas in the Ano Nuevo State Reserve there are 7,000 of them. Guided walks are available all year but during the breeding season (December-March) places are limited.

## FURTHER INFORMATION

For guaranteed UK seal sightings look at **www.sealtrust.org.uk**, **www.cardiganisland.com**, **www.seescotlanddifferently.co.uk**, **www.clovelly-charters.ukf.net** Tel: 01237 431 405 and **www.ramseyisland.co.uk** Tel: 01437 720 285. For trips to Blakeney Point see **www.beansboattrips.co.uk** Tel: 01263 740 505. Tourism Thanet operates a summer boat service to see seals on Sandbanks close to Ramsgate **www.tourism.thanet.gov.uk** Tel: 9870 2646111. For the Ano Nuevo State Reserve near San Francisco see **www.parks.ca.gov/?page_id=523**. For information about the Monk seal see **www.monachus.org**.

## Some questions to ask

✓ Can we see the seals on foot?

✓ How close can we approach?

✓ How many passengers on the boat?

✓ How certain are sightings?

✓ Will there be food/drink?

✓ Are there toilets?

✓ Is there anybody to explain what we see?

## Why is this good for families?

It's easy to get fairly close to seals and you don't necessarily need to go in a boat.

## Pros

● There's something rather cuddly about seals.

## Cons

● If on foot beware of getting cut off by the tide.

## Where to go

Scotland, Northumberland, the Wash, Pembrokeshire, California.

## When

Common seals are normally solitary so best seen during the June-July breeding season; grey seals only come ashore in the UK and Ireland for the Oct-Nov breeding season (Feb-March in the Baltic).

## Price Guide

You can go on foot for free in some places; Beans boat trips are £7 for adult and £4 for children under 14. If you want to stay close to where there are seals then an all inclusive holiday might cost from £250 a week.

---

### Animals In Captivity

There are some very strong arguments in favour of well run zoos and parks. Top of the list, we'd say, is to help us all develop an empathy for creatures whose fate in the wild we might not otherwise care about. But so many zoos are not well run. Indeed, the conditions in some are appalling. That's why we support the Born Free Foundation which campaigns on behalf of animals in captivity and why, in this book, we're only describing opportunities to see *wild* animals in the *wild*. If, on a day trip or holiday, you're distressed by the condition or treatment of wild animals in zoos, parks, circuses, entertainments or photo opportunities anywhere in the world you should contact the Foundation. See **www.bornfree.org.uk**.

If you fancy doing a bit of good for animalkind at the same time as taking your family on holiday, then consider renting Cnoc na Gaoithe (the Windy Hill to you and me). This two bedroom modernised 19th century crofters cottage on the wildlife rich Isle of Skye – about seven miles from Portree – is on offer through Born Free with the proceeds from rentals going to the Eilean Ban Trust which aims to safeguard Skye's sensitive habitat. Prices from £320 up to £500 for the week. Sleeps up to seven **www.bornfree.org.uk/ukwcot.htm** Tel:01403 240170.

## Unusual Family Holiday No. 3: The Bird Buzz

Birds usually provide children with their first contact with wild creatures. Thank goodness, they're still to be seen all around us, often inspiring a lifelong passion, as the one million plus members of the Royal Society for the Protection of Birds prove. If your children take an interest in garden birds, perhaps assuming responsibility for the feeder, then bird watching weekends and holidays could be the next step. There are plenty of destinations and operators to choose from. Generally it's best to go for adventurous locations, spectacle (large birds or large numbers) and destinations that offer other things to do.

### Tips On Young Twitchers

- Every member of the family should have a pair of binoculars. No doubt fashionable colours will come into it, but on the technical front a 7x50 model is about ideal (that's to say, a magnification of 7x with an object lens of 50mm).

- Youngsters have a disinclination to sit still for any length of time so limit any static hide type bird watching.

- Have a bird identification book with you as well as a camera equipped with a telephoto lens.

- Create extra excitement by having competitions for who spots what first or who logs the greatest number of species.

Watching seabirds can provide all the right ingredients – large birds, huge noisy colonies, adventurous hiking and a beach to play on. Rhum is home to tens of thousands of Manx shearwaters; Orkney to guillemots, kittiwakes and razorbills; Shetland to whooper swans; Atholl to ospreys; and the Gower Peninsula to Brent geese, to name just a few locations.

The autumn migration provides another kind of spectacle. Some 22,000 migrating raptors pass through the Col d'Orgambideska in the Pyrenees each autumn, including short toed and booted eagles, black and red kites, and honey and common buzzards. Gibraltar is another excellent place to watch the show.

South Florida in the springtime dazzles with its nesting bald eagles, grey kingbirds, sandhill cranes, burrowing owls, red-cockaded woodpeckers and many others. Just a one hour drive from Florida's Disney complex is Prairie Lakes where the greatest number of bald eagles nests in the continental United States. Here there are full on organised packages with specialists guides.

---

### Bird Hunting

Hundreds of millions of migrating birds are shot for 'entertainment' each winter, especially in France, Portugal, Spain, Italy, Malta, Greece, Cyprus, the Middle East and North Africa. Permitted target species include thrushes which in Britain are now in serious decline, but even protected species are often shot as well by hunters who are careless or simply don't care. If you're planning a bird watching holiday in a Mediterranean country ask the national and local tourist offices why it's permitted to kill the birds you wish to see. Raise the matter with your MEP. You may also like to join the Royal Society for the Protection of Birds (see below).

---

## FURTHER INFORMATION

The starting point for all information is the Royal Society for the Protection of Birds **www.rspb.org.uk** Tel: 01767 680 551; over 100,000 youngsters are also members – see **www.rspb.org.uk/youth**. Follow links to 'family holidays' for the RSPB's huge list of activity and wildlife packages. The website is full of news, advice and campaigns plus links to equipment sellers such as **www.eagleoptics.com** (for those brightly coloured binos) and good books such as *The Children's Guide to Bird Watching*.

Other useful websites include **www.wildlifeextra.com**, **www.birdsofbritain.co.uk**, **www.birdinguk.com**, **http://birding.about.com**, **www.fatbirder.com**, **www.scotland.com/bird-watching**, **www.birdforum.net**, **www.myfwc.com**, **www.parks.ca.gov** and **www.saltonsea.ca.gov**. See **www.travel-quest.co.uk** for links to specialist holiday companies.

## Some specialist operators

**www.birdfinders.co.uk** Tel: 01258 839 066

**www.heatherlea.co.uk** Tel: 01479 821 248

**www.walescottages.com** Tel: 01792 864 611

**www.midwalesbirdwatching.co.uk** Tel: 01970 890281

**www.seescotlanddifferently** Tel: 0870 760 6027

**www.responsibletravel.com** Tel: 01273 600 030

**www.explore.co.uk** Tel: 01962 733 051

## Some questions to ask

✓ Is this holiday suitable for children?

✓ Will there be a lot of static viewing?

✓ What birds are we likely to see?

✓ Is the programme flexible so we can do our own thing?

✓ What will the weather be like?

✓ What equipment should we bring?

## Why is this good for families?

Birds are about the easiest wildlife to watch and can start children on the road to nature appreciation in all its forms – what's more, the holiday can continue in your own back garden afterwards.

## Pros

• If the next generation doesn't have respect for the environment, we're lost.

## Cons

• Too much sitting and standing for some children.

## Where to go

Where not? From your back garden to the back of beyond there are birds to look at. Particularly celebrated locations (at the appropriate time of year) include the Scottish Highlands and Islands; the Col d'Orgambideska in the Pyrenees; the Balme, Bérard, Golèze, Bretolet, Hahnenmoss and Voza passes in the Alps; Gibraltar, Malta, the Dardanelles and Florida.

## When

Mostly the breeding season, and the migration season (usually September and October). But some birds (for, example, the bee eater in Spain) can only be seen in the summer and others only in winter.

## Price guide

Package trips start from around £350 and go up to over £1,500, including flights, accommodation, food and a guide. But almost any holiday can become a bird watching holiday with the addition of a pair of binoculars.

# Unusual Family Holidays No. 4: The Magic Of Mammals

It's relatively easy to see wild birds but, unfortunately, much harder to spot wild land mammals. So promising to take children to watch the red deer or the wild boar can end up with frustration for everybody. The solution is to consult with the experts. Either book with a specialist company or, if you prefer to go it alone, at least take specialist advice before making your arrangements.

It's a sad fact that in Europe we've destroyed or decimated so many of our large mammals. But there are still some left, if you know where to look:

**Wolves**. In 1970 there were just 500 wolves left in Spain but the numbers have now risen to 2,500 or more, most living in the southern foothills of the Cordillera Cantábrica to the east and west of León. Get out at dawn and dusk.

**Red Deer**. The largest deer in Europe, weighing up to 340kg. Impressive herds on Rhum, Mull and in the Loch Broom area.

**Wild Boar**. Hunters have ensured a plentiful supply in various European countries including France, Germany and Spain, by feeding wild populations and encouraging interbreeding with domestic pigs. Dusk.

**Beaver**. Although it's been decided not to reintroduce beaver to Britain, they can be seen in France, on the Rhone.

**Marmots**. Cute, furry burrow dwellers that can be seen in summer, high in the Alps and Pyrenees. Often give themselves away by their warning whistles.

**Genet.** Gorgeous, nocturnal relative of the mongoose with spotted cat like body and long, banded tail. Try the Albera range of the Spanish Pyrenees, the Monfragüe natural park in Spain's South Meseta and the Sierra de Ancares in north-west Spain. You'll need to go at dusk with a powerful torch.

**Lynx**. Spain's population is down to, maybe, 150 adults, mostly in the Coto Doñana and the Sierra Morena. Try September when dry conditions keep the lynx close to the few sources of fresh water.

**Chamois**. Alps, Pyrenees. In summer they stay high; in the evening they climb towards the summits to get the last of the sun.

**Ibex**. Alps; Spain's Sierra de Gredos and Puertos de Beceite. Usually on rocky, inaccessible ledges.

**Mouflon**. Alps, Eastern Pyrenees. Easily identified by their tightly curled horns, the mouflon have been reintroduced so hunters can shoot them. It's a sad world!

**Otters**. Orkney. Loch Broom area.

**Crested Porcupine**. Sicily. Spectacular creature covered in sharp black and white quills. Dusk.

We can't stress too much that the whole secret of success is to take advice from local people whose directions can be relied upon. Just like humans, animals are to be found in some places (possibly in large numbers) but not in others that look just as suitable. It's also a question of knowing *how* to spot animals whose coats often camouflage them. Until you've got the hang of it, an experienced guide is a good idea.

## FURTHER INFORMATION

Put 'nature holidays' into your search engine, or the name of the particular beast you want to see together with the name of your destination. In the UK, many prime wildlife habitats are owned by the National Trust **www.national-trust.org.uk** Tel: 01704 878 591. You'll find visits to otters, wildcats and the odd dormouse at **www.mtuk.org** Tel: 020 7498 5262. For general information see **www.wildlifeextra.com**. For Florida, the Florida Fisheries and Wildlife Commission (**www.myfwc.com/recreation**) has details of masses of wildlife reserves and sanctuaries with skunks, beaver, opossum and barking tree frogs to name but a few. For California take a look at **www.parks.ca.gov** and **www.saltonsea.ca.gov**.

## Some specialist operators

**www.naturalist.co.uk** Tel: 01305 267 994

**www.naturetrek.co.uk** Tel: 01962 733 051

**www.wildlife-encounters.co.uk** Tel: 01737 218 802

## Some questions to ask

✓ Is this holiday suitable for children?

✓ Will there be a lot of early starts? Late finishes?

✓ What's the chance of seeing the animals we're interested in?

✓ Is this going to be physically demanding?

✓ What clothing and equipment will we need?

✓ What happens in bad weather?

## Why is this good for families?

Everybody loves wildlife.

## Pros

● Giving wildlife an economic value through holidays helps conservation. What's more, getting back to nature restores perspective and develops the spirit (and, very often, the calf muscles, too).

## Cons

● You can never guarantee seeing what you've come for.

## Where to go

There are ibex to be seen behind the Côte d'Azur, mouflon not so far from the beaches of the Côte Vermeille, wild boar behind the Costa Brava, roe deer behind the Costa del Sol, lynx in Andalucia, and wolves in the Spanish Steppes (north of Valladolid). In Florida and California the huge range of mammals includes beavers, coyotes, wild cats, bobcats, elk and skunks. In

Britain, the best places for watching mammals are in Scotland, especially the Cairngorm National Nature Reserve, Mull and Rhum.

## When

Depends what you want to see.

## Price guide

Nature holidays tend to be relatively expensive because you have to pay for one or more specialist guides, plus (sometimes) off road vehicles and boats – and the organising companies are usually quite small. In Europe, £1,000 for 10 days to a fortnight, all included, is quite normal. For an all inclusive nature holiday to California expect to pay twice that.

# Unusual Family Holiday No. 5: Up Close And Personal

Wonderful as it is to see animals and birds in the wild, most of us (and children especially) would like to have some meaningful contact or, at least, get close. As in the films, we'd like to dance with wolves and swim with dolphins. These kinds of things are possible with captive animals but, as we've explained, we're not promoting the keeping of wild animals in captivity in this book. So is it possible to get 'up close and personal' with wild animals? The first thing that has to be said is that there are laws against chasing animals to cuddle them although, in this crazy world, you can still chase them to kill them. But, on the other hand, an animal such as a dolphin can always chase you. Such encounters can be life changing experiences (as we'll see in Chapter 13).

But let's begin with some wild creatures it's relatively easy to get close to here in the UK. Badgers, of course, live in systems of tunnels known as setts. Now, although they're nocturnal they very easily become accustomed to artificial lighting which means that, with a well concealed hide close to the sett, you can watch from only a few yards and see very clearly. Farmers are often the enemies of badgers but, in fact, quite a few have discovered that badger watching can provide a useful income and have developed some marvellous facilities. Take a look at **www.badgerwatchdorset.co.uk** (Tel: 01300 345 293) and for the Banbury area **www.badger-watch.com** (Tel: 01295 780 352).

In the nature reserve behind the beach at Formby, just north of Liverpool, the red squirrels are so tame they may come right up to you if you sit very still **www.nationaltrust.org.uk** Tel: 01704 878 591.

As regards birds, the Wildfowl & Wetlands Trust's headquarters at Slimbridge, Gloucestershire, has hides from which you could almost reach out and touch them. It's a particularly important reserve for Bewick swans. The wintertime floodlit feeds are highly recommended **www.wwt.org.uk** Tel: 01453 890 333.

But to get back to dolphins... Occasionally, solitary dolphins deliberately seem to seek out human contact. Freddie, who befriended people at Amble, was one of those. In other cases, a pod of dolphins becomes used to human interaction over a period of time. Monkey-Mia, in Western Australia, is the most famous example. But, in either case, the procedure is the same. Never chase dolphins because, apart from anything else, you'll drive them away. Instead, just float calmly in the water and the dolphins, if they wish, will come to you.

Swimming in the wild with dolphins is not something to be undertaken lightly. There are no accounts of dolphins attacking people but a careless flick of a tail could (and sometimes has) caused a lot of damage. Rather safer for children are manatees.

Manatees are the sloths of the underwater world which makes them the perfect wildlife encounter. No way will these gentle monsters disappear at speed and there's no risk of attack, either. When winter comes on in Florida (say, mid-October to the end of March) they gather at Crystal River where the water remains a pleasant 72 degrees Fahrenheit year round. Amazingly, you can snorkel with them and just generally hang out. It gives a whole new meaning to: 'Hey, how you doin', Man?'

If none of this is close enough for you then the thing to do is to get involved in wild animal rescue on a working holiday.

Facilities on these kinds of holidays vary enormously, as do the prices – from the frankly expensive down to the very little – so take your time choosing. Some of the organisations concerned are simply delighted to have the help while, at the opposite extreme, others try to make a profit from working holidays (which all goes to help the cause). Accommodation and instruction are usually the only things included. You normally have to make your own travel arrangements and provide your own food. Sometimes you'll wonder if they really want you to come at all. Dedication helps. So not the most pampered of holidays – but, probably, the most memorable and usually for the right reasons.

## FURTHER INFORMATION

Quite a large number of organisations now offer this kind of experience. Take a look at **www.support4learning.org.uk** for extensive links. For the USA try the national parks (**www.nps.gov/oia/topics/ivip.htm**). Read very carefully what's on offer and, if possible, speak to the person in charge on the ground. Don't leap at the first thing. Compare. Problems can arise over the contradiction between the words 'working' — what the charity or scientific body wants — and the word 'holiday', which is what you want. Be clear in your own mind what you're actually willing to do, how much free time you want and the standard of accommodation you're willing to accept.

### Some specialist operators

**www.wildlifesailing.com** Tel: 01227 366 712

**www.wildandfree.co.uk** Tel: 0845 345 9052

**www.responsibletravel.com** Tel: 01273 600 030

**www.birdsunderwater.com** Tel: 800 771 2763 from USA only

**www.discoverycove.com** Tel: 00 1 407 570 1428

### Working holidays

**www.wildwings.co.uk** and click 'ecovolunteers' Tel: 0117 965 8333

**www.earthrestorationservice.org** Tel: 00 33 4 68 26 41 79

**www.greenvol.com** Tel: 01767 262 560

**www.earthwatch.org** Tel: 01865 318 831

**www.btcv.org** Tel: 01302 572 200

**www.i-to-i.com** Tel: 0870 333 2332

### Some questions to ask

✓ Is this suitable for children?

✓ How close can we get?

✓ Is there any danger?

✓ Do we risk harming the animals?

✓ Can we choose what conservation work we do?

✓ Will we actually be working with the animals or doing something else?

✓ Will we have our own rooms?

✓ What is the average age of volunteers?

✓ How much free time will we have?

✓ Do we need any vaccinations to be in close touch with these animals?

✓ What insurance should we have?

## Why is this good for families?

Close contact with animals is good for the spirit and gives a reward for protecting the environment.

## Pros

- Close contact with wild animals can be a life changing experience.

- On working holidays you'll get instruction in techniques related to wildlife such as feeding and tracking.

## Cons

- You may not get to see or touch anything.

- Conditions on wildlife working holidays can be basic and the work physically demanding.

## Where to go

To swim with dolphins, Florida. Working holidays include Iberian wolves at the sanctuary at Mafra in Portugal, monitoring monk seals at Karaburun in Turkey, ringing birds in Italy, counting whales off the Canary Islands or checking wild mustangs in California.

## When

That entirely depends on the animal and the project.

## Price guide

Organised badger watching costs from just a few pounds. Prices for wildlife working holidays vary enormously, depending on the policy of the organisation, the amount of instruction needed to be given and the costs involved in the work that's being done. The price, for accommodation only, could be as little as £100 a week working, for example, at an animal sanctuary. At the other end of the scale, on a high cost project like whale monitoring, the price could be as much as £750 for two weeks — with travel and food on top. For swimming with dolphins in Florida think in terms of over £1,000, excluding flights.

## And finally

Britain's only two herds of reindeer range free on the Cairngorm Mountains near Aviemore and on the Glenlivet Estate about 30 miles away. But they're not so wild that they don't appreciate a little human company and, given luck, you may be able to stroke them **www.reindeer-company.demon.co.uk** Tel: 01479 861 228

# Chapter 2

# Cities With Sand

**Unusual family holidays in this chapter: Barcelona, Athens, Rome, New York, Paris and London.**

Modern youngsters like cities. They feed on the energy, the buzz, the concentration of things to see and do, and, most of all, the opportunity to spend their holiday money on some 'cool' gear in the shops and then be seen hanging around in it.

But, as our survey clearly shows, they like beaches more than anything. So a whole week in a city is unlikely to go down very well. What's more, city breaks are hard work for parents. There's none of that beach style dozing with half an eye open while the kids entertain themselves. Or maybe there is...

Here we tell you how to combine the city with the beach. So don't set off on any of these city breaks without packing your cossies.

And remember that we're only describing the unusual things – you can get the usual things from a standard guidebook.

## Unusual Family Holiday No. 6: Barcelona

When it comes to cities *and* sand Barcelona is top of the list. It's not just any old sand. It's Mediterranean sand. Which also means sun and clear, warm sea. Well, fairly clear. After all, this is a big city. But the water is tested daily and invariably gets the thumbs up.

What makes Barcelona so great is that the beach is right *there*. No long ride on a bus or the underground. The most central is the Platja (beach) de la Barceloneta. When you get tired of swimming and lying in the sun you just pull on a pair of shorts and flip flop your way along the Port Vell marina back to the land of shops and museums. Another whole stretch of beach begins in front of the Olympic Village. In all, you get two and a half miles of sand. Plus Picasso, Gaudí, Miró, La

Sagrada Família, the funfair at Tibidabo, the museums and gardens of Montjuïc and much more.

## 10 Unusual things to do in Barcelona

1 Ride the *Transbordador Aeri*. A lot of tourists see the cable cars spanning the harbour but not so many actually ride on them, partly because they don't seem to go anywhere useful. But they make a great bribe. The kids agree to spend a few hours at the museums on Montjuïc in return for the ride down to the Platja de la Barceloneta for a swim. The cable cars are so high (the central tower is over 500 feet tall) that it's like flying. Single tickets around £5.50; return around £6.50.

2 Hug a tree. After you've visited the Parc d'Atraccions del Tibidabo be sure to take a stroll in the forests of the mountain itself, the Serra de Collserola. Just 15 minutes from the very centre of the city, there are about 10 million trees here, plus 1,000 different species of plant and around 190 species of invertebrates. Most important of all, these 8,000 hectares are estimated to release 60,000 metric tons of oxygen every year and eliminate 80,000 tons of carbon dioxide. So give those trees a pat. They're doing a great job. If you want to learn all about it, take the one-hour walking tour (Saturday mornings) **www.parccollserola.net** Tel: 00 34 93 280 3552. Also on the mountain is the Carretera de les Aigues, a more or less flat three mile track with tremendous views over the city and much favoured by Barcelona's joggers.

3 Watch birds. Barcelona's Parc de la Ciutadella is more than just a nice green spot to eat your sandwiches. For in the trees high above your heads is the largest heronry in Spain and the largest urban heronry in Europe. The story goes that a single heron escaped from a cage in the zoo in 1970 and was joined by a wild mate. Other escapees which can be seen include little egrets, the rare glossy ibis, and noisy monk parakeets which are multiplying fast, not just in the tall palm trees of Barcelona but in other Spanish cities as well. You might also like to visit the Llobregat Delta Nature Reserve, an important wetland habitat close to the El Prat Airport – it has a nice beach, too.

4 Watch a castle being built. The Catalans have a strange national sport – building human castles. Known as *castellers* these folk practise several evenings a week and at weekends give public displays of their skills. Barcelona's *castellers* are renowned for being partic-

ularly brave with the number of 'storeys' they build. Most Sunday mornings you can see them in the Placa d'Ajuntament, accompanied by the quintessential *gralla* (pipe) and *timbal* (drum). Outside teams are often invited to compete and the whole event can be quite exciting as the final piece of the castle – a child who scrambles to the top – gives a rapid victory wave and slithers down again **www.castellersdebarcelona.org** Tel: 00 34 93 498 2728.

**5** Take a boat trip on a *golondrina*. The boats leave from near the Columbus Monument either to tour the port (about £3) or to run up the coast past Port Olympic (about £7) **www.lasgolondrinas.com** Tel: 00 34 93 442 3106.

**6** Jog up the tunnel onto the pitch at Barcelona Football Club. It's all part of the tour of the club's museum and stadium, including the changing rooms, the dugouts, the press room, TV studios and directors' area. Camp Nou is in Av Aristide Maillol, about three miles to the west of the city centre. Adults around £8, children around £5.50 **www.fcbarcelona.com** Tel: 00 34 93 496 3608. The official place to buy match tickets is **www.barcelona-football-club.com** Tel: 00 34 615 967 283.

**7** Visit a hospital (without even being ill). Hospital Sant Pau is a UNESCO World Heritage Site. Designed by Lluis Domenech i Muntaner, one of Europe's leading Modernists, it was officially opened in 1930, an extraordinary mixture of stone, marble, brick, ceramic and mosaic. To find it, walk along Av. Gaudi from the Sagrada Familia and in about 10 minutes you'll come to the unmistakable building in c/St Antoni Maria Claret. It's still a working hospital but there are guided tours in English daily at 10.15 and 12.15 **www.santpau.es** Tel: 00 34 93 256 2504. Also **www.rutadelmodernisme.com**.

**8** Make a chocolate soldier. Or any other figure you fancy. The Barcelona Chocolate Museum (Museu de la Xocolata) also has tastings and confectionery workshops. This is one museum the kids may ask to go back to. Around £2.50 to get in; workshops extra. At c/Commerc, 36 **http://patisseria.com** Tel: 00 34 93 268 7878.

**9** Tour Barcelona by bike. For four hours your guide will lead you, mostly on cycle paths, through parks and along narrow, traffic free streets. About £16 **www.fattirebiketoursbarcelona.com** Tel: 00 34 93 301 3612.

**10** Tour Barcelona on rollerblades. Barcelona has caught up with Paris (see below). Friday nights are for all comers. Thursday nights are for keenies. Tuesday nights are for the insane **www.patinar-bcn.com** and **www.barcelonainline.com**.

Barcelona Metro runs daily 5am-midnight and until 2am Friday, Saturday and Sunday. Families should either buy the *T-familia* which gives 70 trips for around £25, or the two to five day passes which cover metro, bus and some urban train journeys.

## FURTHER INFORMATION

For general information contact Barcelona Tourist Office **www. barcelonaturisme.com** Tel: 00 34 93 285 3834 (the main office is underground at Placa Catalunya). Also see **www.bcn.es** and **www.barcelona-tourist-guide.com**. For city tours see **www.cruisingbarcelona.com** Tel: 00 34 605 948 469 and **www.rabbies.eu.com** Tel: 00 35 93 211 9566. For unusual experiences see **www.lifestylebarcelona.com** Tel:00 34 93 270 2048. For holiday apartments try **www.athome-barcelona.com** Tel: 00 34 62 936 9950. To book hotels try **www.perfectsuntravel** Tel: 0871 720 2063.

## Unusual Family Holiday No. 7: Athens

Our number two choice of a city with sand would be Athens. Unlike Barcelona, the water isn't right by the city centre, but it's close enough in the port area known as Piraeus. We'd recommend you do your swimming a tad further afield, however, in the resorts of Glifádha or Voúla which are nowadays more or less the southern suburbs of Athens. Either stay by the archaeological sites and commute to the coast for a swim, or stay on the beach and commute to the sites. Vouliagméni, a little further on, is smarter but still no more than 30 minutes by car from the town centre. On the East side of the peninsula, Schinias Beach, close to Marathon, is less than an hour's drive from Athens. Renowned for the shade of the pines that come right down to the beach it's popular with windsurfers. For details of bus departures from central Athens Tel: 00 30 21 0821 0872.

### 10 Unusual things to do in Athens

1 Ride the coastal tram. Opened in 2004 these high tech trains will take you from Syntagma Square in the city centre out to Glifádha

for the beach. Try to get in the first carriage for the view out of the front window.

**2** Soak in Lake Vouliagméni. A geological curiosity, the brackish, mineral laden waters are replenished from underground streams making the lake 50cm higher than the adjacent sea at Vouliagméni beach resort.

**3** Bike round Athens. Take in the Ancient Agora, the Roman Agora, the Theatre of Dionysus and much else during this five mile, two hour circuit. It's the environmental way to see a city whose ancient monuments are gradually being dissolved by car exhausts **www.pamevolta.gr** Tel: 00 30 210 675 2886.

**4** Go to an outdoor cinema. After all, you don't get many of those in Wigan. Most films are in the original language, usually English (with Greek subtitles) but, in any event, watching the film is only part of the experience. We'd recommend the rooftop above Brettos Bar and Distillery on Kydatheon in the Plaka district (where parents might care to sample the home distilled ouzo). Also the Aegli in Zappiou Gardens where the atmosphere is always lively **www.aeglizappiou.gr/cinema.html** Tel: 00 30 210 336 9369. Don't forget to buy some *passatémpo* (pumpkin seeds).

**5** Buy something from the Monastiraki Flea Market (every Sunday) in the streets around Lfesto and Pandrosou. But if anyone offers you a statue without arms be very careful.

**6** Buy sandals from the 'poet sandalmaker of Athens'. Stavros Melissinos has made sandals for John Lennon, Sophia Loren, Jackie Onassis and Anthony Quinn who played Zorba The Greek in the sixties film. His poetry, plays and essays have been translated into several languages but he says he still makes sandals because 'a writer needs first hand experience'. His shop is at 2, Aghias Theklas Tel: 00 30 210 321 9247. While there, take a look at Number 11 where Lord Byron lived for a time.

**7** Ride the funicular to the top of Likavitós, enjoy the view to Piraeus and (on a clear day) the islands, and then walk back down through the woods.

**8** Put on headphones at the Museum of Popular Musical Instruments. You can see *santoúris, bouzoukis* and all the rest and hear the sounds they make in the hands of experts. How cool is that! The museum is at 1-2, Diogenes (in the Plaka district) **www.culture.gr** Tel:

00 30 210 325 0198. Any small boys who still want to be train drivers might also enjoy the Athens Railways Museum, Siokou St. Well, it makes a change from ruins and statues **www.culture.gr** Tel: 00 30 210 490 3163.

**9** Eat a statue. At GelatoMania on Takis Street the ice cream is sculpted. Other Greek gastronomic experiences include Chios mastic from Mastiha, a sort of early chewing gum (and it's considered very good for ulcers) **www.mastihashop.com** Tel: 00 30 210 363 2750. And rather than a bag of crisps buy a bag of *loukoumades* – freshly cooked little doughnuts covered with syrup and cinnamon. There's a good café on the 6th floor of the Eleftheroudakis book shop in Panepistimiou St **www.booksgr** Tel: 00 30 210 322 9388.

**10** Stroll in the king's private gardens. Now they're open to the public as the National Gardens at Leofvas Amalias St, 1 (7am-sunset). There's a children's playground as well as a Botanical Museum and a café Tel: 00 30 210 721 5019.

## And two things nearby

The Peania Caves, just a couple of miles out in the limestone massif of Mount Ymittos, are an awesome spectacle of stalactites, stalagmites and columns Tel: 00 30 210 664 2108.

Mount Parnitha National Park covers 300 square kilometres and is some 20 miles north. Here are over 800 types of flora and fauna, hiking trails and 20 limestone caves, home to people in prehistoric times. Plenty of animals (deer, rabbit, fox, badgers and jackals) as well as birds. For organised tours see **www.alternativegreece.gr** Tel:00 30 210 933 7037.

---

When taking the Metro look out for the displays of archaeological finds discovered during the excavation of the tunnels. Syntagma Square and Acropolis are especially interesting.

---

For cheap admission to all the ancient sites, go first to the Acropolis and buy the Euro 12 multi-ticket which includes the Ancient Agora, the Temple of Zeus, the Roman Agora, the Theatre of Dionysus and the ancient cemetery of Keramakis. (If you don't buy it at the Acropolis you'll have to buy separate admissions at each site.)

## FURTHER INFORMATION

For the Greek National Tourism Organisation see **www.gnto.gr** Tel: 00 30
210 870 7000. For Athens information Tel: 00 30 210 331 0392.
For general information see **www.greektourism.com** and
**www.wordtravels.com**. For museums and sites see
**www.greek-museums.com** and **www.culture.gr**. For private tours and travel
arrangements see **www.tourtripgreece.gr** Tel:00 30 210 942 4468.

# Unusual Family Holiday No. 8: Rome

Every child should be taken to Rome at least once. Its history and its
sites will leave an indelible impression. But however much imagina-
tions are stirred by the Roman Forum and the Coliseum and gladiatorial combat there will come a time when the beach beckons. In ancient
times Rome was a lot closer to the sea than it is now but, even so, the
Mediterranean is no more than a 30 minute drive from the centre (or
take the train from Magliana metro station). In fact, Rome's Fiumicino
Airport is more or less on the beach on the north side of the Tiber while
Lido di Ostia, Rome's main beach resort, is on the south side.

When you haven't got time to get out to the beach, the Piscina delle
Rose is a great outdoor swimming pool (daily May-September) with
plenty of children's activities – Viale America, 20 Tel: 00 39 065 926 717.

For sunbathing everyone goes to the gardens of the Villa Borghese.
There's a boating lake, too. Swimming isn't advisable in the Tiber, but
you can kayak in April/May. There's an organised seven day tour up
river to Citta di Castello for about £70 **www.discesadeltevere.org** Tel: 00
39 329 688 3135. There's also kayaking on the Laghetto dell Eur in the
southern suburbs.

### 10 Unusual things to do in Rome

1 Segway round Rome. It's the only way! A Segway is an electric
powered two wheeled platform on which you stand while controlling
everything via handlebars. After about 30 minutes' practice you
can go at a fast run. Unfortunately this isn't for young children
because you need to weigh 45kg but strong teenagers are going
to love it. It's serious, too – the guides are all experts in art and
history. The three and a half hour tour takes in all the major
sites including the Coliseum and the Roman Forum. About £50
**www.segwayfirenze.com/rometours.asp** Tel: 00 39 06 860 6173 or
**www.segwayexperience.it** Tel: 00 39 05 529 1958.

**2** Skate round Rome. Unlike the mayhem of Paris on a Friday night (see below) you don't have to be experts for this one. Just turn up around 9pm in the Piazza del Popolo with your own (or hired) rollerblades. You can get lessons on Sunday mornings, too **www. pincio.com**.

**3** Bike round Rome. You probably wouldn't dare on your own but in an organised group and with an experienced guide it all seems perfectly safe. In three and a half hours you'll take in all the highlights such as the Coliseum, the Piazza Venezia and the Spanish Steps. Around £14 if under 26, otherwise around £18 **www.enjoyrome. com/walking/bike.html** Tel: 00 39 06 445 1843.

**4** See Rome underground. That's where a lot of the best stuff is. Dungeons are always popular with kids and you can't beat those below the Mamertine Prison. At the Church of St Clement you descend three levels and through two thousand years of history seeing a 4th century basilica and an ancient temple dedicated to Mithras. Under the 5th century Basilica of St John and Paul are recently excavated Roman houses with frescoes **www.tours-italy. com** Tel: 00 39 041 520 8616. To see the most recent excavations below the Vatican Basilica you'll have to send an email to **uff.scavi.@fabricsp.va** or **scavi@fsb.va** giving the size of your party, the date you want and the language you need. Further information from **www.vatican.va** Tel: 00 39 066 988 5318 (no children under 15). And at the Coliseum make sure you include a tour of the labyrinth of corridors and rooms beneath the ground where the shows were prepared. Even lower (but not yet open to the public) archaeologists have unearthed the bones of the unfortunate animals – tigers, bears, giraffes and many others – killed in the name of entertainment **www.romasoteranea.com** (in Italian) or **www.underrome.com** Tel: 00 39 328 902 6924.

**5** Still with an underground theme, visit Rome's catacombs. The Christian catacombs are the most extensive and date from the 2nd century until the 5th. Because Christ was buried, the early Christians rejected the pagan cremation and it was far cheaper to excavate tunnels than to buy land. During the persecutions they were used for the celebration of the Eucharist. There are three main catacombs: Catacomba di San Callisto – the largest (closed Wednesdays and all February); Catacomba di San Domitilla, the oldest (closed Tuesdays and all January); and Catacomba di San Sebastiano (closed Sundays and mid-November until mid-

December). Guided tours are available from the entrances **www. catacombe.roma.it** Tel: 00 39 065 130 1580.

**6** See where Keats died. Not everything in Rome is Roman. The so called Keats-Shelley House is right by the Spanish Steps, the part of the city that has attracted foreign artists and writers from Goethe to Oscar Wilde. Unchanged since the poets' time, the house is now a museum with an extensive collection of paintings and manuscripts relating to Shelley, Keats, Byron (who lived nearby), Oscar Wilde, Wordsworth, Robert Browning and Elizabeth Barrett, including a reliquary containing a lock of her hair and that of Milton. Around £1.50 (children under six free) **www.keats-shelley-house.org** Tel: 00 39 06 678 4235.

**7** See ghosts. A town like Rome should have plenty of them. This walking tour starts from the Piazza Navona at 7pm and lasts three hours. About £25. **www.viator.com**.

**8** See the Angels And Demons sites featured in Dan Brown's less famous book. About £40 **www.angelsanddemons.it** Tel: 00 39 338 500 6424.

**9** Go on a spending spree with a personal shopper. This is one for the girls, really. It's not cheap but in a city like Rome your personal shopper could save you money (and she takes you in her own car). Around £165 for a half day; around £265 for a full day **www. shopping-rome.it** Tel: 00 39 339 214 2009.

**10**Tour the ancient lavatories of Ostia Antica. Always a winner with children. Ostia Antica is the stop before the beach and in Roman times was the harbour town. Well preserved by mud, it rivals Pompeii. The public lavatory block has running water and seating for 20 – sponges on sticks served as loo paper. But there's a lot more to see than just that. Open 9am until around sunset; entrance around £3.50.

## FURTHER INFORMATION

For general information try **www.enjoyrome.com** Tel: 00 39 06 445 1843.

For private tours try **www.romearound.it** Tel: 00 39 067 045 0346 or **www.rometour.it** or **www.odysseytours.com**.

## Unusual Family Holiday No. 9: New York

As everybody knows, New York is one helluva town. But not everybody realises it's also a town with beaches. You never see them in TV series or films set in New York but they're there. After all, Manhattan is an island. In fact there are miles of them. Apart from Coney Island (see below) you'll find about three-quarters of a million New Yorkers enjoying Rockaway Beach on a summer weekend (in the Gateway National Recreational Area). Wealthy New Yorkers make the 80 mile journey out to the Hamptons **www.hamptons.com**.

### 12 Unusual things to do in New York

1 Kayak round New York. How different can you get? **www.manhattankayak.com** Tel: 00 1 212 924 1788.

2 Bike round New York. You get a whole day with a guide in front and a 'protector' riding at the back for around £40 **www.toursbybike.com** Tel: 00 1 201 837 1133. Or just do a couple of hours in Central Park for around £23 for adults and £12 for children under 16 **www.centralparkbiketour.com** Tel: 00 1 212 541 8759.

3 Hover over New York. You'll never find a cheaper (or shorter) helicopter ride than this. The helicopter takes off from Paulus Hook Pier for a ride that lasts around 150 seconds – but, then, it only costs about £16 **www.libertyhelicopters.com**.

4 Learn to fly through the air with the greatest of ease. Without either a helicopter or a plane. And the Trapeze School of New York gives you great views of the Statue of Liberty while you're doing it **www.trapezeschool.com** Tel 00 1 917 797 1872.

5 Take a ride on the Staten Island Ferry (it runs 24 hours a day and it's free).

6 Buy a toy at Fao Schwarz Toy Store. If you arrive early you'll catch the opening ceremony then ride the Motion Simulator and interact with the fantasy characters who roam the building **www.fao.com** Tel: 00 1 10153 0023.

7 Go to a, err, museum. But the kids will love these. Believe us. Try the Children's Museum of Manhattan, 212 West 83rd Street Tel: 00 1 212 721 1234; the Staten Island Children's Museum, 1000 Richmond Terrace **http://statenislandkids.org** Tel: 00 1 718 273 2060; Museum Kids (part of the famous Metropolitan Museum of Art) **www.metmuseum.org** Tel: 00 1 212 570 3961; and Forbes Collection

at 62 5th Avenue, including 500 toy boats and 12,000 toy soldiers **www.forbescollection.com** Tel: 00 1 212 206 5548. All the family will enjoy the Sonywonder Technology Lab which is packed with inter-active exhibits. And, what's more, it's free. 56th Street and Madison Avenue **http://wondertechlab.cony.com** Tel: 00 1 212 833 8100

**8** Visit scenes from your favourite films and TV shows such as *Sex And The City* and *The Sopranos* **www.screentours.com** Tel: 00 1 212 209 3370.

**9** Immerse yourselves in the largest Chinese community in the Western hemisphere. New York's Chinatown, within sight of the Empire State Building, begins where Grand and Mott Streets inter-sect and is home to 150,000 people. There are shops selling every kind of Chinese product and more than 200 Chinese restaurants.

**10** Eat at Mars 2112. This has to be one of America's best theme restaurants. You arrive via a simulated space journey and, once you've landed, naturally there are 'Martians' mingling with the din-ers. Arcade games keep the kids entertained while the adults linger over coffee. 1633 Broadway **www.mars2112.com** Tel: 00 1 212 582 2112. Also try the Jekyll & Hyde where there's a show for kids and parents every half hour 91 7th Avenue South **www.jekyllpub.com** Tel: 00 1 212 989 7701. You can save money and eat from food carts just like the tough guys do in the movies; try Daisy May's Chili Carts on Broadway at 39th Street, Sixth Avenue at 50th Street and near 40 Wall Street. If you want to eat and sightsee at the same time, amble along on a guided food tour of various New York neigh-bourhoods such as Greenwich Village or Chelsea Market/Meat-packing District. Around £23 **www.foodsofny.com** Tel: 00 1 212 209 3370. If anybody has an American Girl Doll you can all take it (or should we say 'her'?) to lunch at American Girl Place on Fifth Avenue **www.americangirl.com** – if you haven't got the doll they'll lend you one.

**11** Go to Coney Island on the south side of Brooklyn and visit the amusement parks, such as Astroland **www.astroland.com** Tel: 00 1 718 265 2100 or Deno's Wonder Wheel **www.wonderwheel.com**.

**12** Hike through the wetlands of the Jamaica Bay Wildlife Refuge, part of the Gateway National Recreation Area, just a few minutes from the hubbub of Brooklyn **www.nps.gov/gate** Tel: 00 1 718 354 4606.

## FURTHER INFORMATION

Tour operators to New York include **www.completenorthamerica.co.uk**
Tel: 0115 950 4555 and **www.virginholidays.co.uk** Tel: 0870 220
2788. For general information see **www.sogonow.com**, **www.nyc.com**,
**www.newyorkkids.net**, **www.nyctourist.com**, **www.theinsider.com**.
For advice from those who have already been see **www.virtualtourist.com**
and **www.tripadvisor.com**. For New York's parks see **www.nycgovparks**.
For news of what's on see **www.wirednewyork.com**,
**http://nyc.freecityevents.com** and **www.nymag.com**. For city tours see
**www.trustedtours.com** Tel: 00 1 305 433 8395. For hotel rooms try
**www.roomsnet.com/newyork** or **www.quickbook.com** or
**www.affinia.com**.

---

If you're staying in New York for a week get a Seven Day Unlimited Ride
MetroCard, covering the subway and buses. It costs around £13. Up to
three children 44 inches tall and under travel free when accompanied by a
fare paying adult.

---

## Unusual Family Holiday No. 10: Paris

Paris is no longer the city of the Eiffel Tower but the city of
Disneyland. As such, it's on every child's agenda. But how can there be
a beach when the sea is over 100 miles away? Zay are vairy cleverr,
zees Frainch! Every summer since 2002 Paris has had a beach two
miles long, complete with palm trees, sun loungers and volleyball. And
there's always somewhere to swim (but not in the Seine itself).What
they do is import some 2,000 tons of fine sand and spread it along what
is normally a road by the river. Which means you can make sand castles but just don't try digging down very far.

### 10 Unusual things to do in Paris

1   Segway round Paris. There's no better way of taking kids on a tour
    of Paris than the Segway. It's the kind of personal transport you'd
    expect Captain Kirk and Mr Spock to use. Believe us, once the kids
    have seen a Segway nothing else will ever do. The Segway is an
    electric powered platform on two wheels which is (more or less) self-
    balancing. You stand at the controls and glide effortlessly past
    pedestrians at a good running speed. And you get a great commen-
    tary as well. But, unfortunately, not suitable for small children.

Tours last four to five hours. Around £50 **www.citysegwaytours. com/paris** Tel: 00 33 15 658 1054.

**2**  Skate round Paris. If you feared the kids would refuse to go sight-seeing ever again without a Segway then worry not. There are always rollerblades. Rollerblades have become a Friday night institution. At 10 pm around 15,000 *patineurs* assemble at the foot of the Tour Montparnasse (near the station) and there's about as much excitement as anybody can handle as speeds reach 30mph. This is certainly not for the fainthearted or beginners or young children **www.pari-roller.com**. Somewhat easier are the Sunday afternoon outings that start at 2.30pm from 37, Boulevard Bourdon, close to the Place de la Bastille, which are open to all **www.rollers-coquillages.org**.

**3**  Bike round Paris. Less futuristic than a Segway, less thrilling than rollerblades, bikes are nevertheless highly practical. And dodging the traffic on a bicycle, with or without a string of onions, will keep a little bit of spice in your lives. Around £17 **www.fattirebiketoursparis.com** Tel: 00 33 15 658 1054.

**4**  If your kids are fans of the Doors they'll surely want to pay homage at the grave of Jim Morrison. It's in Père Lachaise which has been *the* place for celebrities to be buried ever since 1803 when Nicolas Frochot bought land on the hill known as Champ l'Evêque and in a smart piece of marketing had Molière, La Fontaine and Abélard and Héloise dug up and reburied there **www.pere-lachaise.com**.

**5**  Go down the drain. If the kids have seen or read Victor Hugo's *Les Misérables* they might be intrigued by the idea of visiting the sewers into which Jean Valjean fled. A section has now become the Paris Sewer Museum and the entrance is at Pont d'Alma in front of 93 Quai d'Orsay **www.paris.org/musees/egouts/info.html** Tel: 00 33 14 705 1029.

**6**  Enter the underworld. The Paris catacombs were begun 2,000 years ago for the quarrying of limestone, but from 1785 onwards millions of bones and corpses were buried and stacked in the 200 miles of galleries. You'll walk less than a mile in a tour that takes two hours. Locals in the know have ways of getting in for raves and parties, assuming they can evade the *cataflics* – the special police. The entrance is near Metro Denfert-Rochereau **www.showcaves.com** Tel: 00 33 14 322 4763.

**7**  Even today's kids are well aware of the Second World War, thanks to a constant TV diet of films and documentaries. If they and you have ever wondered what it must have been like to live under Nazi occupation then take the World War II Walk. Around £8. The same organisation will also take you around the Da Vinci Code sites for around £15 – meet in front of the Ritz Hotel in Place Vendome where Robert Langdon was staying when the book opened **www.classicwalksparis.com** Tel: 00 33 15 658 1054.

8   See a Paris fashion show. Boys may or may not be interested but girls will certainly be enthusiastic about this one and it's free at the famous Printemps store on Boulevard Haussmann. Every Tuesday at 10am in the auditorium on the 7th floor **http:// departmentstoreparisprintemps.com** Tel: 00 33 14 282 5787.

9   Visit the Jardin d'Acclimatation in the Bois de Boulogne. This is what Paris had before Disneyland and in its own way it's still very good. There are little trains and boats and cars and ponies to ride on, mini golf, bowling, dolls and all the traditional things. Entrance is around £2 and each attraction then costs around £1.50 **www.jardindacclimatation.fr** Tel: 00 33 14 067 9082

10  See the puppet show at the Marionettes des Champs-Élysées at avenues Matignon and Gabriel.

---

It's cheaper to buy 10 Métro tickets at a time – ask for a *carnet* and you'll save about 25%. For unlimited travel for one day buy a *Mobilis*. For up to five days buy a *Paris Visite* – children from four to 11 are half price and children under four are free.

---

If you want to see a lot of museums buy a *Carte Musée et Monuments*. It allows you to visit 65 as many times as you can manage in one, three or five consecutive days.

---

## FURTHER INFORMATION

**www.paris-touristoffice.com** Tel: 00 33 83 668 3112

## Unusual Family Holiday No. 11: London

As Dr Johnson, the famous 18th century writer and wit, famously remarked, when a man is tired of London he's tired of life. And he might have said the same of a child, too.

## 18 Unusual things to do in London

1 Bike Round London. The guides know the quiet roads and the parks that will take you to Buckingham Palace, Trafalgar Square, the Houses of Parliament and all the rest. The Royal West Tour covers nine miles in a leisurely three and a half hours and costs £16.95 **www.londonbicycle.com** Tel: 0207 928 6838.

2 Skate round London. If you're not all clued up about rollerblades then you might need a lesson or two first in Battersea, Kensington or Hyde Parks. For a family of four you'll pay £12.50 an hour each **www.citiskate.co.uk** Tel: 0207 228 2999. After that you'll be ready for the free Sunday afternoon outing which starts on Serpentine Road at 2pm **www.rollerstroll.com**. And after *that* you'll be ready for the real thing, the Friday Night Skate which starts at Hyde Park Corner – for starting time and other information see **www.thefns.com**.

3 Boat round London. A boat trip from Westminster Pier to Kew takes an hour and a half. Return ticket £16.50 adults; £8.25 children. Information 020 7930 2062. Kew has plenty for children, including a Climbers and Creepers playroom; adults £11.75; children under 17 free **www.rbgkew.org.uk** Tel: 020 8332 5655. A Hopper Pass with Catamaran Cruisers allows you to 'hop on' and 'hop off' all day long on the River Thames for £19.75 for adults and £10.25 for children under 16 – and the price includes a 'flight' on the London Eye. Other sites you can easily visit from the river include the Houses of Parliament, Tate Modern, Shakespeare's Globe Theatre, St Paul's Cathedral, the Tower of London and the National Maritime Museum at Greenwich **www.catamarancruisers.co.uk** Tel: 020 7987 1185.

4 Amphib round London. Amphib? Well, we didn't know what else to call riding in an amphibious vehicle. But that's what you do. You begin at Waterloo and take in famous sites such as Buckingham Palace, Downing Street and the Houses of Parliament before trundling down a slipway and continuing the tour along the River Thames. Duration: 70 minutes. Adults £17.50; children 13-15 £14; children under 12 £12. **www.londonducktours.co.uk** Tel: 020 7928 3132.

5 Wall wedge round London. No doubt you admonish your children to 'walk properly' at frequent intervals. But if you take a stroll with artist Lottie Child you'll get urban street training. Which means

she leads you around London, demonstrating such moves as the wall wedgie, the spinning pig's tail and the two step stand. Walking with your children will never be the same again **www.malinky.org**.

> If you insist on using such banal transport as tubes, buses and the Docklands Light Railway don't forget to buy a One Day Travelcard. One adult with a Travelcard can take four children under 11 for free and it costs just £5.40 after 9.30am.

**6** Visit London's haunted houses, graveyards and the scenes of Jack the Ripper's Whitechapel murders.
Price £6.50 **www.london-ghost-walk.co.uk** Tel:020 8530 8443.

Or you can do your own macabre walk by strolling more or less due west from Newgate Street to Marble Arch via Holborn and Oxford Street. You'll be retracing the route of the carts that for 500 years until 1783 took condemned criminals from Newgate Prison (later the site of the Old Bailey) to Tyburn gallows. Which is where the expression 'going west' comes from. Along the way, make a point of looking at number 285 High Holborn, once the Blue Boar pub, where Oliver Cromwell personally intercepted a secret plan from King Charles I, sewn inside a saddle.

**7** If the kids are moaning by the time you get to the site of the gallows at Marble Arch don't let such talent go to waste. Give them a box to stand on and let them join all the others railing against the iniquities of life at Speaker's Corner (Sunday mornings only).

**8** Jog up the tunnel onto the pitch at Chelsea football stadium. Unfortunately the aspiring footballers in the family won't be getting paid millions. On the contrary, the cost of the privilege is £13 for adults and £7 for children, including a 75 minute tour of the whole place **www.chelseafc.com** Tel: 0870 603 0005.

**9** See the never, never house. Numbers 23 and 24 Leinster Gardens, Paddington, W2 are one of those curiosities kids tend to find quite fascinating. The five storey façades with their columns and balconies looks normal enough. Why, there are even plants in the window boxes! But knock on the doors and no one will ever answer. Because the houses are dummies, just five feet thick. And behind is the Metropolitan Line, the world's first underground railway.

**10** Stroll around Spencer House, London's most magnificent private palace, built for an ancestor of Diana, Princess of Wales in 1756-66.

At 27 St James's Place, it's been breathtakingly restored to its late 18th century appearance. Open Sundays (except January and August) from 10.30am-5.45pm **www.spencerhouse.co.uk** Tel: 020 7514 1958 (Children 10 and over only), £9.00.

**11** Greet Boudicca at Westminster Bridge. It took the English artist Thomas Thornycroft almost 30 years to complete Britain's most enthralling statue of the Queen of the Iceni. But the kids may be even more intrigued by the little doorway in the base, the entrance to a tunnel leading to the Bank of England.

**12** Buy an antique at Bermondsey Market. The tourists go to Portobello, the professionals go just south of Tower Bridge on Friday mornings. Make sure you get there before 7am if you want to beat them to the bargains **www.visitsouthwark.com/ bermondsey-antiques-market**.

**13** Set the kids the task of finding the Sherlock Holmes Museum. It's really quite elementary. Clue: Holmes used to live at 221b Baker Street. (Second clue: **www.sherlock-holmes.co.uk** Tel: 0207 935 8866.)

**14** Admire London's lesser known but hugely impressive art collections at the Courtauld Institute at Somerset House, Aldwych (famous for its Impressionists) **www.courtauld.ac.uk** Tel: 0207 848 2777 and the Wallace Collection in Hertford House on Manchester Square **www.wallacecollection.org** Tel: 0207 563 9500.

**15** Enjoy culture on the cheap. Free lunchtime concerts at St Paul's Cathedral, St James's Church, St Martin in the Fields, the Queen Elizabeth Hall foyer and (Saturdays) the National Theatre foyer. Opera is nearly free if you stand at the Royal Opera House (from £4) **http://info.royaloperahouse.org** Tel: 0207 304 4000 or English National Opera (£5) **www.eno.org** Tel: 0870 1450 200. For reduced price theatre tickets see **www.officiallondontheatre.co.uk/tkts/today**.

**16** Arm yourselves with a portable encyclopaedia of biography and see who can spot the most famous names at Kensal Green and Highgate Cemeteries. In the former you'll find the graves of the engineer Isambard Kingdom Brunel, the novelists Wilkie Collins, Anthony Trollope and William Makepeace Thakeray, the mathematician Charles Babbage and more than 550 other notable figures. Guided tours every Sunday at 14.00 **www.kensalgreen.co.uk** £5 (children under 12 not admitted to the catacombs). Highgate is very different, having been named as London's spookiest cemetery and said to have inspired Bram Stoker, author of Dracula. Here you'll find the graves of Karl Marx, George Eliot, Christina Rossetti and Michael Faraday. Guided tours every day **www.highgate-cemetery.org** £5 (minimum eight years old).

---

The London Pass gives access to 60 attractions including the tour of Chelsea football stadium and Kew Gardens: £29 for an adult and £18 for a child **www.londonpass.com** Tel: 01664 485 020.

---

**17** Spot the celebrities. Whenever you're in London there's always a chance of seeing celebrities, especially on the King's Road and Knightsbridge. The problem is that you can just never be sure where they're going to be at any moment. But happily for you we've come up with a solution. Turrah! Meet the film stars you can always count on...

**Tower Bridge** starred in *Lara Croft: Tomb Raider* with Angelina Jolie, *The Mummy Returns*, and most memorably of all *Brannigan* when John Wayne's car only just managed to leap the widening gap between the two halves. Incredible timing!

**The Millennium Dome** appeared in *The World Is Not Enough* when James Bond fell onto it from a balloon. But it was only a supporting role.

**Repton Boys Club, Cheshire Street** starred in *Lock, Stock And Two Smoking Barrels*. But the club's acting has been criticised on the grounds that it was only playing itself, since the notorious Kray Twins used to work there.

**The Painted Hall of the Old Royal Naval College** at Greenwich needs to be treated with deference having starred in *The Madness Of King George, The Avengers, Quills* and *Lara Croft: Tomb Raider*, while the nearby chapel starred in *Four Weddings And A Funeral*. Definitely in the superstar category.

**Borough Market** had the luck to play opposite Renée Zellweger in a Bunny Girl costume in *Bridget Jones's Diary*. Meanwhile, Bridget's flat was just above the nearby **Globe** public house.

**Spitalfields Market** featured in the film version of Dickens' *Nicholas Nickleby*.

**New Billingsgate Market** in Docklands starred in *28 Days Later.*

**The Market Porter** public house in Stoney Street played the 'Third Hand Book Emporium' in *Harry Potter –The Prisoner Of Azkaban* and went almost unrecognised.

But it's **the empty space** near Wapping New Stairs that wins the great acting award for its portrayal of the Lion and Unicorn public house in *The Long Good Friday*. First of all the space was transformed into the pub – and then it was blown up. Such dedication to art!

**18** Eat on the cheap. Take a picnic to Coram's Fields, a seven acre 'secret garden' especially for children, right by the British Museum. We're breaking our rule about not mentioning zoos because the animals here are all domesticated – ducks, hens, sheep, goats and so on. But remember that no adults can enter Coram's Fields without a child, so you'll have to be nice to the little blighters **www.coramsfields.org** Tel: 0207 837 6138. Camden Market has dozens of food stalls for grazers. Open every day from 10am-6pm **www.camdenlock.net**. At the Café In The Crypt, St Martin in the Fields, Trafalgar Square you can get hot and cold self-service meals and snacks **www.smitf.org** Tel: 020 7766 1158. Two restaurants with activity centres are

Babes'n'Burgers, 275, Portobello Road Tel: 020 7229 2704 and Blue Kangaroo 555, King's Road, 020 7371 7622.

### That's all very well but where's the beach?

We were just coming to that. No need to get shirty. London does, indeed, have a beach in front of the Royal Festival Hall. We wouldn't actually recommend swimming, although the river is a lot cleaner than it used to be. Happily, you can do all the other beach things like sunbathing and even, yes, making sandcastles. The Reclaim the Beach movement holds regular summer parties **www.swarming.org.uk**.

If you want to lie on some sand *and* swim then go to the Serpentine Lido in Hyde Park **www.creativearts.com/serpentinelido/** Tel: 020 7706 3422 (adults £3.75 children £0.90).

For a rather different ambience try Hampstead Heath Ponds. One is for women only, one for men only and one mixed. Real enthusiasts (some say nutters) even break the ice here in the depths of winter before setting off for work **www.myhampstead.co.uk**.

If you're not quite that wild, the Hampstead Heath Lido is a civilised, oblong alternative (£4) **www.cityoflondon.gov.uk**.

Hampstead Heath was once notorious for its 'gentlemen highwaymen'. The Frenchman Claude Duval was the first. According to one story he stopped a coach in which there was £400 – a fabulous sum in those days – but kept only £100 after the lady in question agreed to his request to dance with him on the heath. Duval was arrested in 1669 in the Hole-in-the-Wall pub in Covent Garden and hanged at Tyburn. Another who made a point of extreme politeness was the famous Dick Turpin – but even his elegant manners didn't save him from being hanged in York.

## FURTHER INFORMATION

See **www.visitlondon.com**, **www.londinium.com**, **www.london-tourist-information.com** and **www.travelengland.org.uk** Tel: 0800 192 192.

### Pros

- Unlimited activities when not on the beach
- Beach can act as a reward for visiting cultural sites

### Cons

- Higher prices in general
- Possible water pollution

## And finally

Marseille is probably not a place you'd think of going for a holiday. But when it comes to big city attractions by the sea it takes some beating. France's second largest city has some great museums including the Roman docks (*Docks Romains*), an archaeological museum, two history museums, a natural history museum and two important art galleries. The small town beaches tend to get rather crowded but there are plenty more all along the coast. Best of all is the island prison – a 15 minute boat trip – on which Dumas based his famous tale of *The Count of Monte Cristo*. But in real life nobody ever escaped.

# Chapter 3

# Beach Holidays With A Difference

**Unusual family holidays in this chapter: long distance swimming, snorkelling, diving, surfing, windsurfing, dinghy sailing, sea kayaking, beach riding and much more.**

Beach holidays are Number 1 with kids (our survey confirmed that) and with plenty of adults, too. So a beach resort is the obvious choice for a family holiday. But there's a lot more to be done on a beach than simply sunbathe, swim and build sandcastles. So, come on, bin the bucket and spade and try out some of these suggestions.

## Unusual Family Holiday No. 12: In The Swim

Just about everybody swims when they go to the beach so what's unusual about that? Ah yes, but we're not talking about a family holiday with the occasional swim to cool off. We're talking about swimming as the whole *point* of the holiday. We're talking about, maybe, a mile or two every day (say 2-5km).

The first thing, of course, is to be able to cover that kind of distance. If you can't, get training at your local pool or take a look at **www.swimclub.co.uk** and **www.clubswim.com/swimming-camps.asp** for links to specialist holidays, clinics and camps. For one to one holiday teaching see **www.swimwithus.co.uk**.

It really isn't that difficult to build up to a leisurely mile, provided the water is calm, warm and still. Which means the Mediterranean. Even so, take local advice because there can still be dangerous currents.

There are two ways of going about the holiday swimming. *Along* the coast. Or *across* the sea from, say, one island to another.

Probably *along* the coast is the best option for a family. There's not much to organise and if anybody gets tired it's easy to go ashore. All you need to do is choose a suitable coastline. A stretch with lots of small promontories and little bays is ideal. On a hot day with a calm sea you set off from the beach of your hotel, swim down the coast, have lunch then get a taxi back. Next day you take a taxi to your furthest point and repeat the procedure. Once you start to get too far from your hotel, change hotels. It's a wonderful way of getting to know all the little inlets and at the end of the holiday you'll have a real sense of achievement.

---

### Tips: Organising your swim

- You can take money with you in a waterproof container tucked inside your swimming costume.

- Wear a swimming hat to protect your head from the sun and tinted goggles to protect your eyes.

- Apply plenty of waterproof sun lotion.

- Wear waterproof sandals or similar so you can get ashore where it's rocky and walk to a beach restaurant.

---

Even better would be to swim between islands in an archipelago, say in the Cyclades. But that takes a lot more organising. Which is where specialist tour operator SwimTrek comes in. SwimTrek (see below) will take care of all the logistical problems, including a support boat to take all your luggage and to haul family members out of the water and revive them with hot drinks when necessary.

## FURTHER INFORMATION

### Some swimming specialists

**www.swimtrek.com** Tel: 020 8696 6220

**www.holidays.swimmingwithoutstress.co.uk** Tel: 01239 613789

**www.artofswimming.com/holidays.shtml** Tel: 020 8446 9442

**www.swimmingnature.co.uk** Tel: 0870 094 9597

**www.bluewatertrainingcamps.co.uk** Tel: 00 38 631 832 124 or 00 33 687 287 368

## Some questions to ask

✓ Is this suitable for families?

✓ What's the furthest we have to swim in a day?

✓ What's the water temperature?

✓ What happens if one of us can't swim any further?

✓ Is coaching available?

✓ Will we need wetsuits?

✓ What other things are there to do apart from swimming?

## Why is this good for families?

Facing a challenge together keeps a family together.

## Pros

- Healthy.

- Gives a sense of purpose to a beach holiday and motivates improvement.

## Cons

- No place for weak swimmers.

- Needs good organisation.

## Where to go

The tideless Med is a good bet – particularly the Costa Brava, Corsica, the Cyclades, Crete and Rhodes. If you're organising your own swims make sure there's a ferry, bus or taxi for the return trip.

## When

Summer.

## Price guide

Think in terms of around £350 for a SwimTrek weekend and £650 for six days.

A tailor made learn to swim course in Swadlingcote, Derbyshire will cost you around £250 before accommodation.

## Unusual Family Holiday No. 13: Snorkelling

If you can swim you can snorkel. And that adds a whole new dimension to a beach holiday. Suddenly, swimming has a real value to it. It's not just a way of exercising and it's not just for cooling down. It's a way of seeing marine life close up. Far closer, in fact, than you'll generally see wildlife on land. And it's something every swimming member of the family can do. There's nothing difficult about it. Nor is it one of those activities at which you all have to be at the same level. You can all enjoy yourselves in your own way.

You'll need a mask so you can see and a snorkel so you can breathe while your face is in the water. Fins or flippers allow you to cover more sea with less effort and without having to use your arms. Nowadays they come in all kinds of designs and sizes. Boys tend to be attracted by the biggest ones. But remember the bigger (and stiffer) the fins the more powerful your legs need to be. So it's probably best to start out with something modest. Finally, you might need a wetsuit if the water is cold. In the Mediterranean in summer it won't be necessary.

If snorkelling is going to be the main focus of the holiday then it needs to be given a little structure. Equip everyone with an underwater camera (there are single use models that are quite cheap). Have competitions, such as who can identify the greatest variety of fish in a single day. (But don't have competitions about who can go deepest or stay down longest – that's dangerous.) Try snorkelling at night, with underwater torches – you'll see completely different species to the daytime.

What might you see? Well, even if you see nothing else, there's the underwater landscape. But in the Med you're virtually guaranteed common and white spotted octopus, various corals, anemones, sea cucumbers, starfish, bizarre sea potatoes, eels, scorpion fish, venerable grouper, barracuda, colourful rainbow wrasse, the astonishing plate shaped sunfish and ethereal jellyfish.

### Tip: Fitting a mask

A mask should cover your eyes *and nose*. It's essential it fits well, otherwise water will seep in and prevent you seeing clearly. The test is to hold the mask against your face (without using the strap) and inhale through your nose. If the mask is a good fit it should stay in place entirely by the vacuum created. If it falls off then it's a poor fit.

## Tip: How to stop your mask misting up

When you put your face in the water your mask is liable to mist up, just like a car windscreen on a rainy day. There are products you can buy to discourage misting, but there is a cheaper and easier way. Simply spit into your mask, rub the spit evenly over the glass and rinse it out in the water. It sounds disgusting but it works.

## Tip: Getting under the water

Once you've learned to swim it's amazing how difficult it is to get under the water. Don't take too deep a breath (not at first, anyway) because that will make it all the harder. Bending at the waist, push your head and torso down and a moment later throw your legs, held together, up into the air. Their weight will begin to push you under. Capitalise on that impetus by immediately making one or two strong movements with your arms (as for breast stroke). Once your feet are under you can use your fins to power on down. Be determined. It requires a significant effort.

## Tip: Clearing your ears

If you dive down very far under the water (say, 10'/3metres) the pressure will make your ears hurt. And if you continue going down you could actually burst an eardrum. So what's the secret? The trick is to equalise the pressure by squeezing your nose (that's why the part of your mask that covers your nose is made of soft rubber) and at the same time gently exhaling down your nose. The pressure you create pushes your eardrum from the *inside* so it counters the pressure of the water on the *outside*. In the same way, the water pressure will also press your mask against your face; if it hurts simply exhale down your nose to put more air into the mask.

## Tip: Surfacing

When you hit the surface again your snorkel will be full of water. So exhale forcefully, like a sperm whale, to clear the tube.

## FURTHER INFORMATION

There's a little bit more to snorkelling than meets the eye. So it's probably a good idea if everyone has at least one lesson. The best place to get started is your local branch of the British Sub-Aqua Club (**www.bsacsnorkelling.co.uk** Tel: 0151 350 6200). Some diving schools, abroad as well as in the UK, also offer BSAC snorkelling courses. Don't be put off by the fact that most people will be there to learn scuba. Explain that you just want to concentrate on snorkelling. Failing that, at least buy a book on the subject.

For more information on snorkelling and equipment in general look at **www.divemagazine.co.uk** . And price up equipment at either **www.megadivestore.com** or **www.watersportswarehouse.co.uk**. If you'd like to know a bit more about the environmental side of snorkelling (both the good and the bad) then check out **www.reefcheck.org**. To start your search for a specialist operator look at directories such as **www.travel-quest.co.uk**.

## Some specialist operators

**www.adventure-breaks.com** Tel: 01437 781 117

**www.davyjonesdiving.com** Tel: 00 34 69 972 1584

**www.travelaction.co.uk** Tel: 0870 111 7300

**www.keycamp.co.uk** Tel: 0870 700 0740

**www.clubmed.co.uk** Tel: 0845 367 6767

**www.snorkelingcatalina.com** Tel: 00 1 877 510 3175

**www.fla-keys.com** Booking online

**www.activitiesabroad.com** Tel: 01670 789 991

**www.tallstories.co.uk** Tel: 01932 252 002

**www.adventure-sports.co.uk** Tel: 01736 761 838 (winter); 020 8816 7711 (summer)

**www.call2venture.co.uk** Booking online

## Some questions to ask

✓ What's the minimum age?

✓ Can we stay together as a family for snorkelling tuition?

✓ Do we have to take swimming tests first?

✓ Will there be a safety marshal when we snorkel?

✓ Are there any particular dangers snorkelling in this area?

✓ Will we be insured?

✓ Should we bring our own equipment?

### Why is this good for families?

Everyone who can swim can take part at their own level.

The things you'll see will provoke plenty of family discussion.

### Pros

- It's healthy.
- You'll see what goes on in the seven-tenths of the world covered by water (buy a field guide for identification).

### Cons

- Some people get a bit claustrophobic under water (but you can always stay on the surface).

### When to go

It's not a lot of fun when it's cold or storms have destroyed the visibility so June to October tends to be the season in the northern hemisphere (there's also more light when the sun is high in the sky).

### Where

Rocky places have more life than sandy, and the visibility is better, too. In Britain you'll need a wetsuit to enjoy the Scottish Lochs and Islands, Pembrokeshire, Cornwall and the Isles of Scilly as you will Ireland. In the Mediterranean there's excellent snorkelling on the Costa Brava, the Balearics, the Canary Islands, Corsica, Sardinia, the Côte d'Azur, the Bay of Naples, Sicily, Linosa, Corfu, the Aegean…in fact, just about anywhere with a rocky coastline.

### Price guide

Your basic equipment will cost you from £50 up to £250 or even more if you want the very best. Snorkelling tuition will cost about £20 an hour but you won't need much. Otherwise, snorkelling will cost you the same as any other holiday by the sea.

## Unusual Family Holiday No. 14: Diving

At one time we never would have said that diving was particularly dangerous. We'd been doing it for years, on and off, without any problems at all. Then one day an incident occurred, and occurred so easily, that very nearly resulted in a death. You could say that diving is like walking along a wide plank. *Nothing to it!* Except that the plank is above a deep chasm and you have to be very sure you will never, ever trip.

So you have to think very carefully before you introduce your children to the sport. Diving requires characteristics that children don't tend to have in any abundance. Things like attention to detail, taking care of equipment, respect for justified rules and regulations, calm in the face of emergencies. Children tend not to be very meticulous, tend not to take care of things, tend to ignore rules and regulations and tend to be impetuous – all characteristics that can have serious consequences. That having been said, diving *teaches* those very desirable qualities. You just need to be sure your children are the kind who will be receptive to the lessons.

The benefits, in fact, are huge. Diving isn't so much one sport as a gateway to a whole range of possible interests. Apart from it being great fun, diving always involves maths, science and navigation skills and can awaken an interest in all kinds of things such as marine biology, history, the environment, photography and even spirituality.

Probably the best and cheapest way for a family to get started is to join the local branch of the British Sub-Aqua Club (**www.bsac.com** Tel: 0151 350 6200). Age requirements vary from club to club but the minimum is generally 14. Most clubs meet for training one night a week, in the safety of a swimming pool, with weekend activities on top. Over a period of months you can acquire the necessary skills so that, when you go on holiday, you can start 'real' diving straight away and not have to pay for tuition.

Alternatively, if you *only* want to dive on holiday then sign up with a diving school that's well thought of. It's also essential that it gives tuition in English (there's no room for misunderstandings where diving is concerned). BSAC schools do exist abroad (and usually take children from 12) but you're more likely to come across PADI (the Professional Association of Diving Instructors **www.padi.com**). PADI has schools all over the world with courses specifically aimed at the holiday diver and at children as young as eight.

## FURTHER INFORMATION

For general information about diving take a look at: **www.scubaduba.com**. The BSAC has an excellent magazine called *Dive* in which you'll find adverts for holidays in the UK and abroad. For information about diving in Florida take a look at: **www.florida-keys.fl.us/diving.htm** or **www.fla-keys.com/diving/** or **www.floridasmart.com** (and go to diving) or **www.southfloridadiving.com**. For California try **www.caoutdoors.com/Diving_MP.htm**. Information about a dozen or so diving holiday specialists is grouped together on **www.divechannel.co.uk**.

A browse through some of the online directories is a good place to find diving holidays: **www.travel-quest.co.uk**, **www.ukdiving.co.uk**, **www.scubadivingplus.com** and **www.all4kidsuk.com**. If you want to give diving as a present then for £45 **www.intotheblue.co.uk** provides the eight pluses with a 'blowing bubbles' package. For the all important equipment, check out **www.megadivestore.com** or **www.watersportswarehouse.co.uk** or ask your local diving club for the best outlets. Fascinating and important information about underwater conservation can be found at **www.reefcheck.com** and **www.ecofloridamag.com**.

## Some specialist tour operators

**www.oonasdivers.com** Tel: 01323 648 924

**www.scuba.co.uk** Tel: 0800 072 8221

**www.scuba-dive.co.uk** Tel: 01992 815 960

**www.regaldive.co.uk** Tel: 0870 220 1777

**www.barefoot-traveller.com** Tel: 020 8741 4319

**www.clubmed.com** Tel: 0845 367 6767

**www.explorers.co.uk** Tel: 0845 644 7090

**www.diveazure.com** Tel: 00 33 68 072 0410

**www.familydiving.co.uk** Tel: 01285 869 679

**www.davyjonesdiving.com** Tel: 00 34 66 972 1584

**www.itsadive.com** Tel: 00 1 304 453 9881

## Some questions to ask

✓ What certification do you offer (PADI, BSAC etc)?

✓ Do your instructors speak good English?

✓ What's the minimum age for children?

✓ Can we train together as a family?

✓ Will our initial training be in a swimming pool?

✓ Will we be insured?

✓ Where is the nearest decompression chamber?

✓ What sort of dive boat do you have?

✓ Are you equipped with oxygen in case of emergency?

✓ Will there always be someone in charge of the boat when we're diving?

**WARNING**
Diving is a potentially dangerous sport. Take proper instruction. Once qualified we strongly advise you to continue diving with a club or with a certified dive centre and not to dive alone.

## Why is this good for families?

Diving is a big challenge and facing it together as a family builds team spirit and respect for one another. Children can start training at PADI schools from the age of 8; from 10 onwards it's possible to dive with a certified parent or PADI professional to a maximum depth 12m. Diving is a long term sport, not just for one holiday, so it does become part of your lives (and provides plenty of ideas for Christmas and birthday presents).

## Pros

- Teaches qualities useful in life.
- Turns a beach holiday into a real adventure.
- Can spark an interest in all kinds of associated subjects.
- The sea is the best place for getting close to wildlife.

## Cons

- Diving is potentially dangerous.
- Equipment is expensive (see below) and heavy.
- Boring for non-diving members of the group.
- The hotel room will be filled with drying bits and bobs every night.

## Where to go

There are some wonderful places around the UK including the Hebrides, Anglesey, Devon, Cornwall and the Isles of Scilly. Ireland also has some great diving but in northern waters the temperature is, of course, rather cold. In the Med, the Costa Brava, Majorca, Menorca, Ibiza, the Costa del Sol, the

Côte d'Azur, Corsica, Sardinia, Sicily and its islands, Cyprus, Crete and Turkey are all good. Canary Islands waters are cooler than the Med in summer but warmer than most of it in winter. The Florida Keys have the longest living coral reef in the western hemisphere.

## When

Summer – diving is a lot more pleasant when the water is warm, though dry suits have made winter diving tolerable.

## Price guide

Compared with many other extreme sports, diving holidays aren't expensive. In the UK prices start at around £300 for a week (accommodation, air and daily boat dives) while an all inclusive week's holiday in the Mediterranean, including 10 dives, will cost around £750. A PADI Open Water qualification costs around £225 (four days). Escorted dives cost around £20 per dive. The cost of your own equipment (wetsuit or drysuit, buoyancy compensator, regulator etc) is expensive – if you get hooked as a family of four it could all easily cost £5,000.

# Unusual Family Holiday No. 15: Surfing

Surfing has suddenly taken off in Britain. According to the British Surfing Association (BSA), about a million of us are now having a go. Although it's still mostly a male sport, around 100,000 'surf chicks' have proven that women can do it, too. And there are really no age limits. The only requirement is to be a strong and confident swimmer.

If you live in the London area and have teenage children then a good way of testing the water, so to speak, is to get the *Big Friday Surf Bus* which all through the summer leaves London on Friday evening and returns Sunday evening, giving you a weekend in Newquay to have a go (**www.bigfriday.com** Tel: 01637 872512). If you enjoy that then a full scale holiday could be for you.

As beginners you'll want the stability of longboards or Malibus (about eight feet for an adult). Ideally they should be soft boards or 'foamies', which are highly buoyant and very forgiving. But once you've got the hang of things you'll graduate to shorter 'pop-outs' – surfer speak for production line foam boards covered with fibreglass.

The first big problem is standing up on the board – the 'pop-up'. As soon as you've 'caught' a wave (by paddling) you grab the rails (sides), straighten your arms (as if doing a press up) and bring your legs under your body. Speed and smoothness are essential. Practise on the beach first. The second big problem is staying up – pretty tricky when there's no binding to hold you to the board.

At least one of the family should manage the pop-up the first day. Anyone who hasn't managed it after three days might like to switch to kneeboarding (i.e. you stay on your knees) or bodysurfing (i.e. you don't have a board at all).

If you really find it isn't your thing you can always buy one of those cheap polystyrene bodyboards available near any beach these days and float gently around.

## FURTHER INFORMATION

For general information contact the British Surfing Association (**www. britsurf.co.uk** Tel: 01637 876 474). Other useful sites include **www.surfing-waves.com** and **www.surfingholidays.net**. For kneeboarding see **www.kneeboardsurfing.co.uk** and **www.kneelo.org**; for bodysurfing see **www.body-surfing.co.uk**. Useful magazines include *Wavelength, Carve, The Surfers Path* and especially *Coast* which is on DVD. For specialist operators try putting 'surfing holidays' into your search engine together with the name of the destination.

Schools in the UK include Surfer's World, Devon (**www.surfersworld.co.uk** Tel: 01271 890 037); Coast to Coast Adventure Sports, Scotland (**www.c2cadventure.com** Tel: 01368 869 734); and Ma Sime's Surf Hut, Wales (**www.masimes.co.uk** Tel: 01437 720 433).

### Some specialist operators

**www.purevacations.com** Tel: 01227 264 264

**www.surfspain.co.uk** Tel: 01691 649 992

**www.winterwaves.com** Tel: 07734 681 377

**www.atlanticriders.com** Booking online

**www.extremeholidays.com** Tel: 08700 360 360

**www.adventurebug.com** Tel: 00 34 952 894 308 or 00 34 635 817 819

## Some questions to ask

✓ What type of board will we start on? (Complete beginners need soft boards or 'foamies'.)

✓ Is your school British Surfing Association approved?

✓ Will we be insured? (Third Party cover is essential.)

✓ How reliable is the surf?

✓ What height is the surf likely to be?

✓ How many pupils per instructor?

✓ What is the average age of your clients?

✓ Can we learn together as a family?

## Why is this good for families?

The typical surfer is a male mid-20s to 40, but anyone can have a go from, say, around eight to 80. Obviously you need to be a strong, confident swimmer and match the surf to your ability.

## Pros

- Healthy.
- Surfing is cool.

## Cons

- Some risk of getting hurt, especially if anyone gets 'worked' by a 'gnarly' wave.

## Where to go

In the UK North Cornwall is the best, especially Crooklets Beach, Widemouth Bay, Watergate Beach, Newquay, Perranporth, Gwithian and St Ives; also the Gower and Pembrokeshire. In Ireland head for Donegal Bay — in fact, the whole west coast is a paradise. In Europe this is one time you don't want the Med (no surf); go for the French coast around Biarritz and Hossegor, the west coast of Spain and Portugal, Madeira (not beginners), Fuerteventura and Lanzarote (all year). Florida is unreliable but can have good surf during the cyclone season (August-October) and sometimes in winter — try Cocoa Beach and Sebastian Inlet. California is the Mecca — anywhere between Santa Cruz and Half Moon Bay but especially Sandspit, Santa Barbara.

## When

The surf is at its best (that's to say, biggest) in the winter, but as a family of beginners you'll find summer, with its smaller surf, safer and easier. Biarritz has a Surf Festival every July.

## Price guide

Surfing holidays can be really cheap. A 'surf safari' in Portugal is £200–£300 a week including food and accommodation in tents (but not flights). At the other extreme, surfing based at a good hotel in California could cost £1,000 or more for a week. If you want to do your own thing, lessons should cost around £25–£40 a day per member of the family. Hire of wetsuits and boards costs around £50 a week each. If anybody gets really bitten by the surfing bug, beginner's boards start at around £200.

# Unusual Family Holiday No. 16: Dinghy Sailing And Windsurfing

A dinghy is the ideal way for a family to have fun together at the beach. It's great for everyone to learn a new skill and it's great to be able to *go* somewhere – that little cove or island off the coast. And there's always the chance of finding *treasure* when you arrive.

After your initial lessons you'll probably be confined to a flotilla at first but once you've proved yourselves you should be able to explore on your own.

Don't forget that dinghies can capsize, some designs very easily. So for a family that includes young children it's essential to choose something stable above all. It goes without saying that *everybody* should be wearing a lifejacket. The great thing about a sailing dinghy is that a role can be found for everybody – taking a turn at the helm, setting the jib, keeping a lookout, checking the wind and so on.

Older children may be more attracted by windsurfing. It gives them the chance to 'do their own thing' while remaining within limits. But the first hours are pretty discouraging for everybody. And tiring. You're going to fall off a lot. Especially when you try to turn. And having to haul the hinged mast back up each time won't do much for your humour (but it will do wonders for your arms). But gradually you'll begin to get the knack. You'll start knowing how much to angle the mast, how much to let out the sail and how much to lean. Then comes the moment you tack (turn) for the first time without falling off. And suddenly you're hooked.

## FURTHER INFORMATION

For general information try the Royal Yachting Association (**www.rya.org.uk** Tel: 0845 345 0400/023 8060 4100) or, specifically for windsurfing, the UK Windsurfing Association (**http://ukwindsurfing.com** Tel: 01273 454 654). For links to dinghy sailing holidays take a look at **www.jojaffa.com** or put 'dinghy holidays' into your search engine together with the name of your chosen destination. For links to a wide range of windsurfing operators take a look at **www.windsurfingholidays.net** or try putting 'windsurfing holidays' into your search engine together with the name of your chosen destination.

## Some specialist operators

**www.planetwindsurf.com** Tel: 0870 749 1959

**www.crystalactive.co.uk** Tel: 0870 402 0275

**www.extremeholidays.com** Tel: 0870 036 0360

**www.sunsail.com** Tel: 0870 777 0313

**www.neilson.co.uk** Tel: 0870 333 3356

**www.adventurebug.com** Tel: 00 34 952 894 308

## Some questions to ask

✓ How old do you have to be?

✓ What is the pupil to instructor ratio?

✓ Will we be insured?

✓ Do you follow the RYA teaching guidelines (applies to both windsurfing and dinghies)?

✓ Are the winds reliable? What force?

✓ What kind of dinghies are available? (Wayfarers are good for families, Fireballs and 505s for two people, Toppers and one man Lasers for individualists.)

✓ What's the depth of the water? (For novice windsurfers it helps if you can stand up.)

✓ Will we be learning in an area reserved for windsurfers? (It's safer if there are no swimmers, paddlers etc.)

## Why is this good for families?

You can all be together in a dinghy. When the kids are old enough to start asserting their independence you can switch to windsurfing.

## Pros

- Exhilarating.

- You don't need surf.

## Cons

- Gallons of ocean may be consumed before you're competent.

## When to go

Summer.

## Where

For dinghy sailing you really need an interesting coastline or nearby islands that give you somewhere *to go* — the Cyclades and the Dodecanese are perfect. For windsurfing, a lagoon is ideal, as, for example, on the Roussillon coast of France at Port-Leucate and Port-Barcarès. Tenerife, Sardinia, Kos, Corfu and Rhodes are all favourites. If you're good, or think you will be, Tarifa is considered to be the windsurfing capital of Europe, given its strong winds.

## Price guide

All-inclusive windsurfing/dinghy sailing holidays in the Med cost from around £500 a week to well over £1,000 in high season. Tuition is on top — a one day windsurfing course for beginners will cost around £45 each after which you'll be ready to practise on your own. Or you could opt for a series of one hour lessons. If the windsurf isn't included you'll have to pay another £120 or so a week to hire one, rather more for a dinghy.

# Unusual Family Holiday No. 17: Sea Kayaking

Children like kayaks. They're exciting and romantic and they put the whole family on the same level with the seagulls and ducks and anything else you're lucky enough to see. And given that you make no noise (well, hardly any) you'll see a lot. What's more, you can get to little bays and inlets larger craft just can't reach.

In the sea, a kayak doesn't go anywhere unless someone paddles which, over the course of a day, can be pretty hard work. So a child needs to be about eight to make a useful contribution. Also bear in mind that a real sea kayak (as opposed to the sort of open plastic bananas you can hire in most places) is a bit more complicated than a river canoe. It could tip over, which means you'll need a little instruction on how to do an 'Eskimo roll'. Sea kayak holidays, therefore, tend to involve groups, with a support boat for the longer and more challenging itineraries.

## FURTHER INFORMATION

If you want to get a feel for kayaking take a look at **www.jojaffa.com**, which is inspirational. For general information on canoeing in the UK and abroad take a look at **http://playak.com**. It's a good idea to read one of the canoeing magazines such as Canoe Focus (**www.canoefocus.demon.co.uk**).

For links to operators everywhere try **www.responsibletravel.com** and **www.travel-quest.co.uk**.

### Some specialist operators

**www.seafreedomkayak.co.uk** Tel: 01631 710 173

**www.kayakingcb.com** Tel: 00 34 97 277 3806

**www.seakayak-greece.com** Tel: 00 30 228 402 5304

**www.calkayak.com** Tel: 00 1 800 366 9804

### Some questions to ask

✓ Do you have double kayaks?

✓ At what age can a child be a passenger in a kayak?

✓ At what age can a child paddle a kayak?

✓ Will we be on our own or part of a group?

✓ Will there be a safety boat?

✓ What happens if we get into difficulties?

✓ Will we be insured?

✓ What do we need to bring?

✓ Will there be places to buy provisions?

✓ How far each day?

✓ What is the typical age of your customers?

## Why is this good for families?

With a double kayak a small child can simply ride; older children can join in the paddling.

## Pros

- You become part of the environment and get to see scenery hidden from everyone else.

- No noisy engine.

## Cons

- Can be hard work for children.

- You're rather tied to the environs of the beach for everything from shopping to nightlife.

## Where to go

Britain: Cornwall, Cardiff Bay, Pembrokeshire and the Scottish lochs and islands including Loch Long and the Caledonian Canal. France: Brittany and Corsica. Spain: the Costa Brava and Menorca. Italy: Sardinia. Greece: the Cyclades and Dodecanese. Florida: Key West and the Everglades. California: the Mendocino Coast.

## When

Summer.

## Price guide

A week's sea kayak safari in Spain, sleeping on the beach, costs around £300. Accompanied day trips cost around £60. You can hire canoes/kayaks from around £40 a day.

## Unusual Family Holiday No. 18: Beach Riding

If you've ever watched that lovely family film *The Black Stallion* and thought how wonderful it would be to ride along a beach then this is for you. We're not going to say a lot about riding here because that's dealt with in Chapter 6. But what we *are* going to say is that riding along a beach is very special. It's one of the few natural places you can find for a long, unobstructed canter. And to swim somewhere before cantering back adds a whole, extra dimension.

## FURTHER INFORMATION

### Some specialist operators

**www.kimmerston.com** Tel: 01668 216 283

**www.horse-holiday-farm.com** Tel: 00 353 71 916 6152

**www.foxscrofttravel.co.uk** Tel: 01834 831 841

**www.equitour.co.uk** Tel: 0800 043 7942

**www.horse-vacation.com** Tel: 00 1 707 964 7669 Fort Bragg, California

**www.kellyranchinc.com** Tel: 00 1 904 491 5166 Amelia Island, Florida

### Some questions to ask

✓ Do you have horses available for our range of ages and abilities?

✓ What do we need to wear?

✓ Do we need to be insured?

✓ What happens if there are people lying on the beach?

✓ Will we be able to swim at some point during the rides?

### Why is this good for families?

Good for the horse mad and the beach mad at the same time.

### Pros

● Sand is less painful than earth or rock if you fall off.

### Cons

● It's not easy to find a stretch of coast with enough horse riding interest for a week or more.

### Where to go

The Northumberland coast (especially Holy Island) has miles of empty beaches; Sligo, Ireland has even more. For something warmer try Florida or the Mendocino Coast of California.

## When

The beach needs to be empty, so spring and autumn are usually best; in summer it has to be early in the morning.

## Price guide

A two hour beach ride with Kimmerston Riding Centre, Northumberland is £60 for adults and £45/£50 for children. A four day beach riding holiday with Horse Holiday Farm, Ireland, costs about £400 per person. In the USA think in terms of £35 an hour or £165 a day for the riding only.

# More Unusual Things To Do On A Beach

How about giving your kids the traditional British beach experience you had a generation ago? Blackpool Leisure Beach comes complete with rides on everything from donkeys to the ultimate Big Dipper plus ice creams, rock, candy floss, trams, the tower and, of course, the beach itself **www.blackpoolpleasurebeach.co.uk** Tel: 0870 444 5566.

Kids love castles with dungeons and this one, by the beach in Northumberland, has arms and armour, too. When you've finished you can take a boat trip from nearby Seahouses to the seal and bird colonies on the Farne Islands **www.bamburghcastle.com** Tel: 01668 214 515.

# Unusual Places To Stay On A Beach

How about a 13th century tower on Caernarfon's town wall, with a view of waves and fishing boats?
Tel: 01628 825 925 **www.landmarktrust.org.uk**.

The days of just lying on the beach and going to sleep have, by and large, passed. But Florida still allows beach camping. Try Cape Canaveral National Seashore near New Smyrna Beach for what the Americans call 'primitive camping' (but not in the turtle nesting season from April to September). For organised sites try the State Parks such as Jonathan Dickinson, Sebastian Inlet (great surfing, see above) and Tomoka. In Britain there are good campsites close to many great beaches. Try **www.surfparadise.co.uk** Tel: 01271 890 477 (Devon) or **www.pinewoods.co.uk** Tel: 01328 710 439 (Norfolk) or **www.threecliffsbay.com** Tel: 01792 371 218 (Gower Peninsula, Wales).

## And finally

Why not take part in what is claimed to be the biggest beach barbecue in the world? Down in Cádiz, southern Spain, there's football madness at the end of August when, on completion of the hard fought Caranza football tournament, thousands take to La Victoria Beach for a celebratory (or commiseratory) barbecue. All are welcome. Tel: 00 34 95 680 7061.

# Chapter 4

# Parents Chill, Kids Thrill

**Unusual family holidays in this chapter: cruising with children, children's clubs and much more.**

If you haven't already noticed it, adults and children are, well, let's say *different*. It's never easy finding holidays the whole family can equally enjoy. No doubt that's why beach holidays are so popular. In one spot they cater for adults who want to lie inert just as much as for youngsters who have energy to burn. But surely there must be other kinds of holidays on which the adults can chill out and do nothing while the kids get all the thrills they can handle?

## Unusual Family Holiday No. 19: Cruising

A cruise ship is a great place for adults to relax but a terrible place for kids. Full of blue rinses – and that's just the men. Right? Wrong. It may have been true a decade ago but everything has changed. If you want to take it easy while the kids are entertained then a cruise ship is the perfect place. For a start the kids can't go very far. Well, aboard Royal Caribbean's *Freedom*, the largest cruise ship in the world, they could get fairly well lost among the 4,000 other passengers. But that hardly compares with, say, Barcelona or Benidorm. And it probably has to have the greatest concentration of entertainment in the world. If the kids want to learn surfing there's the FlowRider. If they want to learn climbing there's a climbing wall. There's a water park with a waterfall and a river. Why, there's even an ice rink. Plus, of course, all the usual shows. And if you want to be quite sure the kids won't disturb you then you can send them along to one of the children's clubs which basically means you only have to see them for meals.

All of the cruise lines, in fact, run a variety of programmes for children of different ages. They begin with things like colouring, painting, building bricks and singalongs for toddlers and work up to video games, movies, plasma TVs, internet cafés and parties for teenagers. *Disney Magic and Disney Wonder,* which operate out of Miami, are also good choices because you can combine them with visits to Walt Disney World and Disney's private island Castaway Cay.

## FURTHER INFORMATION

Information about a whole variety of cruise lines is available from The Cruise People **http://members.aol.com** Tel: 020 7723 2450.

### Some specialist operators

**http://disneycruise.disney.go.com** Tel: 020 7723 2450 / 00 1 800 951 3532

**www.carnival.com** Tel: 00 1 305 406 4779

**www.celebritycruises.co.uk** Tel: 0845 456 1520

**www.royalcaribbean.co.uk** Tel: 0845 165 8288

**www.thomson-cruises.co.uk** Tel: 08700 602 277

### Some questions to ask

✓ Will there be other children for my children to play with?

✓ What on-board entertainment is there for children?

✓ Are there organised activities for children?

✓ Are they extra or included in the price?

✓ Are there early meals for children?

✓ Can we have connecting cabins?

✓ Is there a babysitting service?

✓ Are specialist staff screened to work with children and medically trained?

### Why is this good for families?

The right ships have the greatest concentration of entertainment to be found anywhere on Earth.

### Pros

• A pretty safe environment (no traffic, no muggings etc).

### Cons

• Seasickness (but it seldom lasts long).

### Where to go

The Med or the Caribbean are the most popular.

### When

Summer in the Med. In the Caribbean there are two high seasons: February to mid-April, and summer (but the later you go the higher the hurricane risk). Of the low season months May is a good bet.

### Price guide

A family of four will pay: around £2,500 for a seven night Mediterranean cruise with Thomson; from £5,200 for a nine night fly-cruise with Royal Caribbean, calling at Cozumel, Grand Cayman, Montego Bay and Labadee, including flights, transfers and one night in Miami.

## Unusual Family Holiday No. 20: Children's Clubs

Children's clubs can be the perfect solution to family holidays. They're a sort of half-way house between having holidays together and having holidays apart. You all stay in the same place but the kids go off and do their thing while you do yours. Cruise ships (see above) are brilliant at that sort of thing nowadays, but there are plenty of other possibilities.

Center Parcs provide the same kind of self-contained, entertainment dense environment. They don't move around like cruise ships but, to add some travel excitement, you can always book one of the 16 continental sites in the Netherlands, Belgium, France and Germany. De Kempervennen near Eindhoven in the Netherlands is popular with British families because it works out cheaper than, for example, Elveden Forest Center Parc in Suffolk, even after allowing for the ferry. What's more, it has a Snowcenter. Less well known in the UK are the Siblu Holiday Parcs of which there are eight in France.

Sunsail has all day kids' clubs at eight locations in the Med and Caribbean. You can start enjoying freedom as soon as your baby is four months and the upper age is 17. Activities include windsurfing, sailing, tennis and mountain biking. Neilson (Greece and Turkey) and Sudwindsports at St Pierre-la-Mer on the French Languedoc coast have similar products. The well known La Manga Club in Spain has what it calls the Mini-Club Fiesta for kids from three months up to 12; older children can indulge in more adult activities such as mountain biking and aerobics.

Sometimes it seems the facilities for the kids are actually better than those for adults. At the 20 plus Club Med resorts worldwide parents are barred from the hip-hop classes, karate, archery and rollerblading. But, come on, there are plenty of things for you, too, such as learning to sail, windsurf, snorkel and dive. Not to mention eat and drink (drinks are almost always included – within reason). And maybe, just maybe, later on junior will show you a few of those hip-hop moves.

At Walt Disney World, Florida, there's all kinds of help with young-sters. The Kids' Night service (Tel: 00 1 800 696 88105 or 00 1 407 828 0920) offers babysitting in your own room at any time of day. The sit-ters are all over 18 years old and qualified. Reservations can be made up to two months in advance. Different hotels on site also have their own services. For example, Camp Dolphin (Tel: 00 1 407 934 4000 Ext 4241) and Camp Swan (Tel: 00 1 707 934 3000 Ext 1006) both provide supervised activities. Kinder-Care, based in the Administration Centre, offers day care on a drop in basis (Tel: 00 1 407 827 5437). If you're staying at the Hyatt Grand Cypress Resort, Orlando ask about Camp Gator.

In fact, just about every large holiday camp will provide parents with plenty of quality time on their own. But where can you go if you don't like that sort of ambience?

Bedruthan Steps, close to picturesque beaches and rocky coves in Cornwall is a hotel not a camp. Nevertheless it's children's clubs are the equal of those offered by much larger resorts. There's a *Chill Out Zone* for teenagers while for younger children there are *Tadpoles, Minnows, Dolphins* and, wait for it, *Sharks*. Early suppers, evening clubs and nannies complete the parental support leaving you free to enjoy the tennis and squash courts, gymnasiums, swimming pools or just doing nothing at all. The famous Gleneagles, Perthshire also wel-comes children, as long as they don't take their buckets and spades into the bunkers. Activities are more country style, including a quar-ter size Land Rover.

There's child friendly and then there's child mad. At the Cavallino Bianco Family Spa Grand Hotel in the *lederhosen* and pasta region of

South Tyrol they almost won't let you in *unless* you have children. The hotel has an average of 13 childminders at any one time.

## FURTHER INFORMATION

Advice on the most family friendly operators can be found at specialist web sites such as **www.forparentsbyparents.com**, **www.babygoes2.com** and **www.all4kidsuk.com**. And, of course, some of the best advice on the subject comes from friends and colleagues who are in the same family boat.

### Some specialist operators

**www.centerparcs.com** (Tel: 00 31 10 498 9754 for De Kempervennen)

**www.siblu.com** Tel: 0870 998 2288

**www.lamangaspain.com** Tel: 0800 093 2792

**www.2.keycamp.co.uk** Tel: 0870 700 0740

**www.clubmed.com**. Tel: 0700 258 2932

**www.virginholidays.co.uk** Tel: 0870 220 2788

**www.thomsonbeach.co.uk** Tel: 0870 165 0079

**www.gleneagles.com** Tel: 01764 662 134

**www.bedruthan.com** Tel: 01637 860 860

**www.hyatt.com** Tel: 00 1 888 591 1234

**www.cavallino-bianco.com**. Tel: 00 39 0471 783 333

**www.neilson.co.uk** Tel: 0870 333 3356

**www.sudwindsports.com** Tel: 00 33 6 85 95 33 34

### Some questions to ask

✓ What childcare facilities are there?

✓ Are childcarers fully checked out, trained and qualified?

✓ Are children grouped according to age?

✓ Are there active options for the older kids?

✓ Are there rest facilities for the toddlers and younger?

✓ Are there babysitting facilities?

✓ Are there separate eating arrangements available?

✓ Is there medical cover for emergencies?

✓ What are the minimum/maximum ages?

✓ Can I get clothes laundered easily?

✓ Do rooms have tea making facilities and fridges?

✓ Do I have to book cots or high chairs in advance — are they an extra cost?

✓ Are there family rooms or suites?

## Why is this good for families?

Parents have time to themselves; children have fun.

## Pros

- Children can develop independence from parents in a safe environment.

## Cons

- Children's clubs usually come together with a holiday camp ambience which you may not like.

## Where to go

Beach resorts are favourite.

## When

Summer.

## Price guide

A family of four can expect to pay: around £1,500 for a fully inclusive week at the Palm Beach Club Hotel in Playa d'en Bossa, Palma, Majorca with Thomson Holidays; around £2,000 for a fully inclusive week at Club Med's Metaponto resort. The Kids' Night Service at Walt Disney World costs from around £8 an hour for one child up to around £12 for four or more. Supervised activities at Camp Dolphin and Camp Swan in WDW cost from about £3 an hour; Kinder-Care costs around £5 an hour or £20 a day.

## And finally

Esprit Holidays runs what it calls its Teen Rangers programme in Chamonix in the summer. For three days (Monday, Wednesday and Friday) your teenage children will be taken off your hands and subjected to such energy absorbing pursuits as ice climbing, snowblades on the glacier, rafting, ice-skating and (rather tame, this) bowling. They'll also get to eat pizzas and fondues. At the end of it all they should be thoroughly *unbounced*. A week in Chamonix with Esprit Holidays costs from £299 each while the Teen Rangers Club costs £169 on top **www.esprit-holidays.co.uk** Tel: 01252 618 300.

# Chapter 5

# Home Alone...
# While The Kids Go

**Unusual (non-)family holidays in this chapter: summer camps, sports camps, summer schools, universities and much more.**

When you think about it, going on holiday as a family is crazy. Would you really want to go on holiday with adults who hate the things you like and like the things you hate? Of course not. So what makes you think your children are any different? Why not just admit the obvious. Adults and children aren't the same. And they don't enjoy the same kinds of holidays.

We're not suggesting you force your children to go on holiday on their own. But we are saying that if your children want to then don't fight them. There's no need to feel guilty. You can be sure they won't be feeling guilty about going on holiday without you. What you're doing whilst they're away is entirely up to you. You could carry on working. You could simply relax at home. Or (this is really sneaky) you could take a holiday as well.

So how do you get the little blig...er, darlings...to agree to go? Well, of course, they may already have thought of it and want to. If not, gently float the idea well in advance by saying something cunning like: 'I hope you won't want to be going on holiday on your own now that you're older. I know those camps can be just the most fantastic fun but we're hoping you'll be joining us on our stamp collecting trip.' If they're a little nervous when the time comes Camp Beaumont has plenty of advice on its website. Also take a look at **www.forparentsbyparents.com** and **www.all4kidsuk.com**.

## Unusual (Non-)Family Holiday No. 21: Summer Camps

American parents have been sending their children to Summer Camps for years so why not you? Mobile phones were invented for this kind of situation.

Camp Beaumont, one of the market leaders, runs five action packed residential centres throughout the UK catering for six to 16 year olds. Most of the wide range of activities are included in the package but you have to pay extra for some specialist courses such as computers and circus skills.

If your kids are more into miming in front of the mirror than white water rafting then PGL offers a Pop Star Holiday. They'll get advice on posture, body language, presentation, singing technique and basic production skills. Then it'll be time to put on the glitter, audition, rehearse favourite songs, take part in the end of course concert and cut a CD to bring back to you – or perhaps send to their agent. PGL also offers an unusually wide range of energy absorbing activities.

You might feel more comfortable with a smaller, family run centre, in which case The Mill On The Brue is perfect. There are 40 activities on site and both parents and children report high levels of satisfaction.

For genuinely athletic kids (nine to 16) Exsportise runs a variety of highly serious courses. On the *Sport and Multisport* programme they can have three hours of professional coaching each morning in their chosen sport (tennis, golf, hockey, soccer, rugby, basketball, netball, swimming or horse riding) followed by a kaleidoscope of sports in the afternoon. Or they can elect to concentrate on just one or two sports. On top of that they can have extra private lessons in the evening including – if it's an Exportise centre abroad – foreign languages.

### FURTHER INFORMATION

#### Some specialist operators

**www.exportise.co.uk** Tel: 01444 444 777

**www.pgl.co.uk** Tel: 0870 050 7507

**www.campbeaumont.co.uk** Tel: 01263 823 000

**www.barracudas.co.uk** Tel: 0845 123 5299

**www.millonthebrue.co.uk** Tel: 01749 812 307

## Some questions to ask

✓ Are all your staff screened for working with children?

✓ What steps have been taken to prevent bullying?

✓ What medical arrangements are in place to deal with illnesses and accidents?

✓ Are there qualified counsellors?

✓ Will boys and girls be sleeping well apart?

✓ Can I contact my child by mobile phone?

✓ Can my child contact me?

✓ How is pocket money dealt with?

✓ Are children allowed out of the camp?

## Which children are summer camps suitable for?

A child needs to be independent and gregarious; even so, it helps if there are two siblings or two close friends to go together.

## Pros

• The kids can have a holiday with other kids even if you can't afford the time or the money to take a holiday, too.

## Cons

• The kids may feel you're getting 'rid' of them.

## Where to go

Camp Beaumont centres are based in London, Norfolk, Staffordshire and the Isle of Wight. PGL has holidays in Scotland, England, France and Italy. Barracudas has 27 locations, mostly in the Home Counties. The Mill On The Brue is based in Somerset. Exsportise centres are at Seaford College (West Sussex), Claysmore School (Southampton), Sevenoaks School, Verneuil (30km from Paris) and Marbella, Spain.

## When

School holidays.

## Price guide

Camp Beaumont holidays cost around £400 a week all inclusive but certain special activities are around £40 extra. The Mill On The Brue charges £425. PGL holidays cost around £400 in the UK and £500 in France.

## Unusual (Non-)Family Holiday No. 22: Summer Schools

Camps are mostly about fun. But there's another whole style which is far more serious. If the kids want to brush up on a subject, play music with other talented youngsters or learn a new career skill then summer *schools* are the answer. They can even go off to university for a bit. Not a bad idea if they can't decide whether they want to do the real thing or not.

Strathclyde University is one of those that takes schoolchildren for a fortnight's summer 'stealth learning' (**www.strath.ac.uk/summeracademy** Tel: 0141 950 3542). Children are said to go back to school with greater motivation and higher aspirations. The Sutton Trust runs summer schools at Oxford, Cambridge, Bristol and Nottingham for Year 12 state school pupils with *non-professional* parents (**www.suttontrust.com** Tel: 020 8788 3223). The students choose one subject and attend lectures and tutorials just like undergraduates. They can also take part in the extra-curricular activities which might include rowing or ice-skating or other things they haven't tried before. Through it all they're guided by an undergraduate mentor. And here's the really good bit. The week on campus is *free*.

It's even possible to go to Oxford or Cambridge. Both institutions run summer schools (**www.cont-ed.cam.ac.uk** Tel: 01954 280 280 and **www.oasp.ac.uk** Tel:01865 793 333) but they're very definitely not free. Prices range from a few hundred pounds up to several thousand when accommodation is included.

If your children are really serious about music then residential summer schools provide the opportunity to interact with other young musicians as well as benefit from different teachers. The Musicale Young Artists' Programme is a three week residential course based in Harpenden, climaxing with a concert **www.musicale.co.uk** Tel: 01582 460978. (Harpenden Musicale also offers five day non-residential 'holidays' all over the country for children from five up to 16.)

If drama is more the thing there's a summer performing arts school in Chiswick, London, which takes children between seven and 17 **www.artsed.co.uk** Tel: 020 8987 6644. There are classes in movement, singing and acting and, on the last afternoon, everything is pulled together into a show for family and friends. Unfortunately there's no accommodation but if you live in the London area then at least the children are occupied during the day. Rather more glamorous is the New York Film Academy which runs courses in Oxford (**www.nyfa.com/summercamps/index.html** Tel: 01865 271 805). And if money's no problem they even have an acting summer camp at Universal Studios, Hollywood. Perhaps Johnny Depp or Sharon Stone will come strolling by. Who knows! Or send the kids on a short course at RADA, the institution that gave us such actors as Diana Rigg and Ralph Fiennes (**www.radaenterprises.org** Tel: 020 7908 4747).

But not all learning experiences are based in classrooms. The Tall Ships Youth Trust will send your teenagers (16+) off on a voyage in UK and foreign waters. They'll learn to scale the masts, set and stow the sails, and take the helm. They'll even learn how to scrub the decks – which could prove a useful skill when they get back to their own bedrooms. See **www.tallships.org** and **www.asto.org.uk** (Association of Sea Training Organisations). If you live in the Torbay area of Devon there's a daytime only summer school for eight to 12 year olds including rock pool rambles, a boat trip and a hike along the coastal path **www.livingcoasts.org.uk** Tel: 01803 202470. And if your kids are fans of Bill Oddie they might like one of the courses run jointly by the Royal Society for the Protection of Birds (RSPB) and the Field Studies Council for 11 to 18 year olds. Keswick, Grange-over-Sands and Betys-y-coed are three of the centres involved. See **www.rspb.org.uk/youth** and **www.field-studies-council.org** Tel: 0845 3454071.

## FURTHER INFORMATION

Put 'summer school' or 'master class' into your search engine together with your chosen subject and the name of your destination. You can see a list of summer schools at **www.summer-schools.info** covering academic subjects, languages, sports, business, music and drama. Details of international music competitions are available from the World Federation of International Music Competitions (**www.wfimc.org** Tel: 00 42 23 21 36 20).

### Some specialist music operators

**www.dartingtonsummerschool.org.uk** Tel: 01803 847 077

**www.uppinghamsummerschool.co.uk** Tel: 01572 820 800

**http://dorsetopera.com** Tel: 01258 840 000

**www.musiceverything.com** Tel: 020 8241 2277

**www.lmfl.com/orchestra.htm** Tel: 01454 419 504

**www.impulse-music.co.uk** Tel: 0118 950 7865

**www.suzukimusic.net** Tel: 01372 720 088

**www.quecumbar.co.uk** Tel: 020 7787 2227

**www.austrian-master-classes.com** Tel: 00 43 66 287 0844

**www.marimbacompetition.com** Tel: 00 32 11 34 87 35

## Some questions to ask?

✓ What level does my child need to be at?

✓ What qualifications do the tutors have?

✓ What sort of accommodation will my child have?

✓ Is the accommodation on campus?

✓ What about meals?

✓ Will anybody be keeping an eye on my child outside of lessons?

✓ Is there any kind of exam/diploma/concert/show at the end?

✓ Are there other activities and entertainment?

## Which children are summer schools suitable for?

Your children need to be serious and dedicated as well as independent.

## Pros

- Tuition of a very high standard.
- The stimulation of fellow enthusiasts.

## Cons

- It's only fun for those children who think work is fun.

## When to go

Summer.

## Where

There are summer schools based at universities and other institutions all over the country.

## Price guide

Think in terms of £300–£400 a week for a typical summer school including accommodation and food (but not transport). Five day Musicale Holiday courses cost around £175 (tuition and musical activities only). A week's summer camp in Hollywood costs around £700 while two week's at RADA will be £1,000 (tuition only). A week's course in audition technique at Chiswick is around £225. The five day 'Living Coasts' summer school is under £100 (10am-4pm). Five or six night residential RSPB courses cost £200–£300.

## And finally

If you worry about your children's safety in or on the water what could be better than a course with the RNLI? They'll not only learn how to look after themselves but how to save others, too, and at the end of their week at Bude in Cornwall they'll have the chance to gain the Surf Lifesaving Association's (SLSA) NOSS (National Ocean Safety Scheme) qualification. But it's not all hard work. There's kayaking, body boarding, surfing, climbing and abseiling, too. The week costs just over £300 including accommodation, food, instruction and use of equipment **www.budesurfingexperience.co.uk** Tel: 0870 777 5111.

# Chapter 6

# Family Activity Holidays (Part One), Keeping Dry

**Unusual family holidays in this chapter: riding, hiking, orienteering, cycling, mountain biking, climbing, ghost hunting and much more.**

As we all know, youngsters have a lot of energy. But rather than directing it at housework and gardening they tend to want to use it to push things to the limit. To provoke dangerous situations unnecessarily. It's a normal, if sometimes inconvenient, part of growing up. Fortunately, most of them (and us) come through with only a few bumps and scratches.

Even so, it makes sense to find positive ways of harnessing that energy. Which is where activity holidays come in. They can provide the challenges that help youngsters to grow up. To cope with life's problems. To have a proper perspective when confronted with difficulties and setbacks. To develop self-confidence. And the very real dangers inherent in sports like horse riding and white water rafting hopefully stop youngsters seeking risks in other unsupervised and secret ways.

There are so many great adventure possibilities that we decided to devote two chapters to them. In this chapter we look at activities on dry land. In the next chapter we'll be looking at those that involve, or at least risk, a soaking.

## Unusual Family Holiday No. 23: Riding

Riding, when you think about it, is a quite extraordinary activity. You sit on a powerful living creature that could as easily kill you by accident as by intent and try to control it. That is where much of the fascination lies and where much of the importance for children's development comes into play. Because a child who understands horses and how to behave around them will have an excellent idea of how to understand people and how to behave towards them, too. That might sound bizarre. Nobody, you might say, should treat a person the way they treat a horse. But turn it round and you can see the sense in it. You *should* treat a horse the way you *should* treat a person. Horsemanship – *modern* horsemanship – isn't about physical coercion and pain; it's about understanding, patience, and about the *self* – self-examination, self-confidence, self-control. Which explains the Arab proverb: The horse is your mirror. With the right kind of teacher it can be a revelation.

So riding is a great activity for youngsters and also for families together and you certainly don't have to be mad about horses to do it.

Probably the best approach for a holiday is to go trekking, that's to say, getting out into the countryside rather than staying in the manège. And there's a style of trekking to suit just about everyone. You could gallop over empty plains or merely walk along mountain paths. You could stay in one place and make day rides or you could have a real adventure, stopping in a different place every night. You could sleep in tents or in luxury hotels. You could look at stately homes along the way or spot wildlife (horseback is a great way to see animals and birds – they don't seem to be so shy of four footed visitors). So it's not just one type of holiday.

And, indeed, there's more than one style of riding. Either you go around like Prince Charles (the English or classical style) or like John Wayne (the Western or cowboy style). We began in the English style but soon realised why cowboys have big, deep, comfortable saddles – they sit in them all day. If you're also going to be in the saddle all day we recommend Western tack (equipment). What's more, children (and anyone a bit nervous) can always grab hold of that nice big pommel in an emergency.

---

### Horseback spectacle

At the Grand Canyon there are mules and horses to take you the hundreds of feet down (and back up) those spectacular cliffs. You can arrange a one hour taster on site or book a week's adventure in advance **www.hiddentrails.com** Tel: 0870 134 4283. Europe's answer is the Cirque de Gavarnie in the Pyrenees, where horses will take you from the village to the foot of the thousand metre high cliffs **www.gavarnie.com**.

## FURTHER INFORMATION

For comprehensive online directories of horse riding holidays of all shapes and sizes in all kinds of destinations see **www.equitour.co.uk, www.riding holidays.com, www.equinetourism.co.uk** or **www.hiddentrails.com**. You can also find holiday listings in equestrian magazines such as *Horse & Rider*. It's important to do some follow up research. Chat on the phone. If you're going to be trekking together you need to be sure that you'll get along.

### Some specialist operators

**www.free-rein.co.uk** Tel: 01497 821 356

**www.angelfire.com/ri/applemore.htm** Tel: 02380 843 180

**www.brenfield.co.uk** Tel: 01546 603 274

**www.criollofarm.com** Tel: 01597 811 353

**www.promenadesdesrieges.com** Tel: 00 33 49 097 9138

**www.ridingholidays.com/discover_brittany_riding_tour.htm** Tel: 00 33 29 789 4030/00 33 29 736 2027

**www.labelleecurie.com** Tel: 00 33 29 998 6631

**www.ranchoferrer.com** Tel: 00 34 95 834 9116/07768 124 572

**www.ranchamerica.co.uk** Tel: 020 7821 4080

**www.canyonrides.com** Tel: 00 1 435 679 8665

### Some questions to ask

✔ Is this holiday suitable for children?

✔ Do you cater for novices as well as confirmed riders?

✔ Will we be able to ride together as a family?

✔ Are there trained instructors riding with us?

✔ Will we be able to try out several horses to find which one suits us best?

✔ What sort of tack do you use (i.e English or Western)?

✔ Are the horses your own or brought in?

✔ Is there something in the area to do other than ride?

### Why is this good for families?

Since it's the horse that does all the work, young and old, fit and unfit, can all get along at the same pace.

## Pros

- Healthy, character building and exciting.

## Cons

- There's always an element of risk around horses.

## Where to go

It all comes down to a question of style. If you want to be cowboys, the USA is the obvious place, especially California's Inyo National Forest, where there are still wild mustang herds. In the UK Exmoor, the Black Mountains of Wales, the Argyll Peninsula and the Highlands around Loch Ness are all good trekking areas. In Europe try the Costa de la Luz, the Alpujarras just behind the Costa del Sol, the Pyrenees, the Massif Central and the Alentejo region behind the Algarve.

## When

In the UK it has to be summer, but horses and hot weather don't go very well together — you'll be plagued by flies — so in southern Europe aim for anything but summer. In California you can ride year round.

## Price guide

Keeping horses isn't cheap and neither are riding holidays but the price range is wide, from around £65 a day upwards, excluding transport. For the *City Slicker* experience on a working cowboy ranch think in terms of £100 a night, but for a luxury 'guest ranch' it could be as much as £1,500 for the week, with flights on top.

# Unusual Family Holiday No. 24: Hiking

Some families absolutely swear by hiking holidays but there's no point in booking one in the mere hope that yours will, too. If you don't do any hiking at the moment there's little sense in going in at the deep end. Try it for a few weekends and if everybody has a great time *then* book the holiday.

Some children like walking, especially if they're allowed to take the lead and be the 'scouts' for the route ahead. Others hate it. You know which yours are. Similarly, some kids like the responsibility and challenge of wearing a rucksack whereas others refuse or compromise by slinging it casually (and ineffectually) from one shoulder. Generally, a fifth of body weight is considered a comfortable load but for children err on the low side.

On a backpacking trip most adults will struggle to carry their own needs, let alone their children's, so it makes sense either to make day walks from a centre or to book the kind of walking holiday in which the tour operator transports the luggage between overnight stops. Then you only have to carry what you need for the day – water, a picnic and some extra clothing. Another solution is to have a donkey or llama carry the gear.

The key to success where children are concerned is the right kind of terrain. Coastal footpaths will probably be the most popular, for obvious reasons. If you can work in a couple of swims per day then it's a perfect itinerary. In the mountains, look for routes that include caves, realistic summit possibilities, and streams or lakes for swimming. Don't aim for the kind of distances you would in an all adult party. Kids can be fast but they don't have much endurance.

Getting the equipment right is tricky. We'd hate to encourage anyone to be irresponsible. On the other hand, legions now set off for an afternoon stroll equipped as if for an Everest summit bid. The more you carry, the slower you go and the more likely you are to get caught out far from civilisation. *Be realistic about your level of fitness.* And don't forget a party can only move as fast as the 'weakest' member, who might be your youngest child. Also be realistic about the degree of comfort you all require. If you've never slept in a tent before then a two week holiday might prove a brutal introduction, especially for anyone anxious about things like make-up.

Whole books are written on the art of backpacking and hiking so here we can't do more than give some basic guidelines. The first is that the whole family needs to be fit before you go. In a one or two week holiday there just isn't the time to build up. If you're not fit you stand a greater risk of injury at the start. Don't bring brand new equipment – make sure everything has been tested and worn in on some hikes at home, especially boots (which might otherwise cause blisters). If you're going without a guide polish up your navigation skills and take with you maps, compass and, if you can afford it, GPS (if you haven't yet caught on to the global positioning system see **http://home.earthlink.net**).

**WARNING**

If you start out as a party then always continue as a party. In other words, don't give in to those faster walkers who suggest: 'We'll go on ahead and meet you there.' Inevitably, someone always gets lost. The rule is: stick together.

## FURTHER INFORMATION

There is a huge number of helpful sites on the internet. The Ramblers Association is a good place to start **www.ramblers.org.uk** Tel: 020 7339 8500. Also take a look at **www.ramblers.org.uk/scotland**, **www.ramblers.org.uk/wales**, **www.walkingpages.co.uk**, **www.traildatabase.org**, **www.walkingworld.com** and **www.hikingandbackpacking.com**. For tour operators see **www.travel-quest.co.uk**, **www.trekamerica.co.uk** and **www.outdoorguide.net**. Be frank with your operator regarding your walking experience and general level of fitness. The John Muir Trust **www.jmt.org** owns or protects important tracts of hiking country, including Ben Nevis and estates on Skye and Knoydart, and has produced a series of itineraries from an hour or two up to several days. Also try putting 'walking holidays' into your search engine, together with the destination that interests you. Useful magazines include *TGO (The Great Outdoors)* and *Country Walking*. Look out for the *Sunflower Landscapes* series of guides which specialises in hikes near popular beach resorts.

### Some specialist operators

**www.inntravel.co.uk** Tel: 01653 617 722

**www.waymarkholidays.com** Tel: 01753 516 477

**www.foottrails.co.uk** Tel: 01747 861 851

**www.ramblersholidays.co.uk** Tel: 01707 331 133

**www.contours.co.uk** Tel: 01768 480 451

**www.scotmountain.co.uk** Tel: 01479 831 331

**www.exodus.co.uk** Tel: 0870 240 5550

**www.responsibletravel.com** Tel: 01273 600 030

**www.mountainandwalking.co.uk** Tel: 01639 831 238

**www.footloose.com** Tel: 1 973 983 1144

**www.llamatreks.co.uk** Tel: 01723 871 234

**www.surreyhills.org** Tel: 01372 220653

**www.llamapark.co.uk** Tel: 01825 712 040

## Some questions to ask

✓ What style of hiking is involved – day walks from a centre, walking from hotel to hotel with luggage transported ahead, or walking in the wilderness and camping overnight?

✓ What facilities (electricity, private rooms, showers, toilets etc) will be available at the overnight stops?

✓ Is this suitable for youngsters?

✓ Do we need to be insured?

✓ What equipment should we bring?

✓ What sort of shoes/boots are appropriate?

✓ Can we rent equipment?

✓ How much will we need to carry?

✓ What distance will we be covering each day – and how much ascent and descent? (If you're not used to mountains an ascent of 300m will add about an hour to walking time on the flat and 1,000m is as much as most people can manage in a day.)

✓ If one of us gets tired can we be transported?

✓ Are picnics included?

✓ Can the children ride the llamas/pack animals?

## Why is this good for families?

Everybody can relate to the great outdoors in their own way but, of course, adults are going to have to make concessions to children.

## Pros

● Non-stop activity and interest.

## Cons

● It might rain.

● If your hiking itinerary involves camping or mountain refuges you're going to have to accept a degree of discomfort.

● If you overdo it you could finish the holiday exhausted.

● Creepy crawlies.

## When

There's nothing more miserable than a hiking holiday in the rain except, perhaps, a hiking holiday when it's incredibly hot. Summer is the only time for
Scotland. The early autumn is best in the high southern mountains (the Alps,
Pyrenees, California's Sierra Nevada etc). Winter and spring can be ideal for
low level treks in the Mediterranean. Check the weather data very carefully
for where you want to go.

## Price guide

Hiking holidays can be very good value *once you've got the necessary equipment*. Going it alone in the wilderness (backpacks, boots, clothing, tents,
sleeping bags and all the ancillaries) could easily cost £2,000 for a family of
four. On the other hand, if you're only day walking between hotels £200 a
head should cover it. As to the holidays themselves, think in terms of around
£500 a week all inclusive up to around £1,000 in high season, with guided
tours costing more than self-guided. If you want a llama to carry your picnic
think in terms of £50 each for a few hours, up to £600–£800 for a week.

## Where

Wherever you choose select an itinerary suitable for the weakest member of
your family party:

**The UK**. Lots of possibilities such as the South West Coast Path; the
Pembrokeshire Coast Path; Offa's Dyke; the Great Glen Way; the Rob Roy
Way, the John Muir Way.

**Ireland**. The North-West Passage from Dublin to County Donegal; the Kerry
Way and Beara Way on the 'five fingers'; the Wicklow Way; the Western
Way.

**France**. A total of 40,000km (25,000 miles) of Grande Randonnée
(GR) footpaths including the GR1, an easy 605km circuit round Paris,
beginning at the château of Sceaux which should take about three weeks; the
GR10 Traverse of the Pyrenees from Hendaye to Banyuls-sur-Mer, a moder-
ate to hard 700km (also possible by the much more demanding 45 day
Pyrenees High Level Route); the GR22-22B, an easy 288km trek from
Paris to Mont St Michel; the GR223 228km coastal walk from Avranches
to Cherbourg; the 841km GR34 tour of Brittany.

**Netherlands**. The Gelrepad among woods, lakes and beautiful countryside in
eight stages beginning at Enschede.

**Belgium**. The GR5A and E9, both of which take you through a variety of scenery along and near the coast; the *Transardennaise*, a 160km route through the forests and meadows of the Ardennes.

**Germany**. The Black Forest, with its 23,000km of footpaths; the Harz and Hochharz National Parks; the Wadden Sea.

**Spain**. The Camino de Santiago, the famous pilgrim route running for 730km from Roncesvalles to Santiago de Compostela; the GR11 Traverse of the Pyrenees from Cap de Creus to Irún in 38 stages.

**Portugal**. The Montesinho Natural Park, home of the Iberian wolf.

**Italy**. The Abruzzo; Tuscany; the Dolomites.

**Greece**. Anywhere in the Pindos Mountains; you might like to have a go at Mount Olympus, at 2,917m the highest in Greece; on Crete the White Mountains and Samariá Gorge.

**Turkey**. The Taurus Mountains and Lakeland.

**USA**. In California it has to be the John Muir Trail, a distance of 211 miles from Yosemite Valley to Mount Whitney, passing through three national parks; in Florida the 1,400 mile Florida Trail.

## Unusual Family Holiday No. 25: Orienteering

So, what is this orienteering so many people go on about? Well, basically, it's a hike or jog on which you get lost, find your way again, get lost again and so on, all the while trying to do it in the quickest possible time to beat the next lot. More specifically, you get given directions (map references and so on) and have to find your way from start to finish with map and compass, being sure to pass through the various checkpoints. So, unlike a normal stroll, it's an organised, competitive event, although plenty of individuals and families just do it for the healthy fun. Most competitors are members of clubs which organise not just day events but whole holidays. Become members and you and your children will be travelling with friends. And around the actual orienteering there are usually plenty of other activities for those with any remaining energy.

### FURTHER INFORMATION

Most orienteering families will be members of a group, club or organisation which will have details of events and travel packages at discounted group prices. But it's not obligatory to travel en masse and DIY details of orienteer-

ing events can be found on any of the many sport's official sites such as:
**www.britishorienteeringfederation.org.uk** Tel: 01629 734 042 or
**www.activitywales.com** Tel: 01437 765 777 or **www.orienteering.ie**
(Ireland). For national events look at **www.orienteeringfederation.org** Tel:
00 358 9348 1211 or
**www.scottishotours.co.uk** Tel: 00 370 6531 0009. In the USA where
there is a growing interest in orienteering try
**www.ultimatetreasurehunts.com**. For mountain bike orienteering take a look
at **www.trailquest.co.uk**. Specialist magazines with full listings and details of
travel possibilities include
**www.orienteeringtoday.com** and **www.compasssport.co.uk**.

## Some specialist operators

**www.henggenting.co.uk** Tel: 0779 559 7252

**www.gringoadventures.com** Tel: 01248 761 177

**www.iain.co.uk** Tel: 01433 650 345

**www.mountainandwater.co.uk** Tel: 01873 831 825

**www.o-travel.com** Tel: 00 34 95 246 0398

## Some questions to ask

✓ Is this event suitable for children?

✓ Is your event, training or holiday linked to one of the sports federations?

✓ Is there anything to do locally other than orienteering?

✓ What equipment should we bring?

✓ What is included in the price?

✓ Are we insured?

✓ What will the weather be like?

✓ Is there trained search and rescue back-up if we get lost?

## Why is this good for families?

Orienteering has evolved as a family activity – you can stay together and play
together for not much more than you'd pay for the travel and accommodation.

## Pros

● Exercise combined with map reading practice.

### Cons

- An activity which is most common off season — therefore think mud.

- Pretty boring for any non-orienteering party member.

### Where to go

In the UK, Wales and Scotland. In Europe, France, Switzerland, Spain and Portugal are also enthusiastic. The sport is just becoming popular in the USA. Most events are in open countryside but a few are urban.

### When

Any time.

### Price guide

Entry fees are usually around £10 but, obviously, travel, food and accommodation are on top. Training camps can cost around £100 a day.

## Unusual Family Holiday No. 26: Cycling And Mountain Biking

Quite a lot of parents are apprehensive about their children cycling. And that's understandable. Most roads in Britain are pretty dangerous places. And you certainly wouldn't cycle on them for *pleasure*. But holiday cycling can be a very different experience, provided you choose your destination – and time of year – carefully.

There are basically three styles. You can stay at a hotel or campsite and make daily outings. You can tour between hotels, leaving it to your operator to transport all your luggage. Or you can do your own thing with bulging panniers. Most operators suggest a lower age limit of 10 or 12 depending on the countryside but usually add that you know your own child best so on your head (or legs) be it. If you have very young children you can tow them in a trailer.

*Cycling For Softies* was one of the first into this market 20 years ago and is still pedalling along (see below). We tested one of their holidays at the time, pottering about in the Beaujolais region from pre-booked restaurant to pre-booked restaurant and pre-booked hotel to pre-booked hotel. Very pleasant it was, too. It can tailor make itineraries for your family and can change plans subject to need midway.

If you're really afraid of the traffic then mountain biking, well away from surfaced roads, could be the solution. But be warned that however much a mountain bike may look like a 'softie' bike the resemblance is entirely superficial. Mountain bikes are for whooshing down steep mountain trails strewn with boulders and loose rocks, leaving strips of skin behind you as you go. Of course, there's no law that says you *have* to do it that way. But people who sign up with specialist operators tend to *want* to. If that's not your thing, look for destinations with plenty of wide dirt tracks from which you can enjoy the scenery without feeling you've been inside a cement mixer. If you fancy giving it a try without dedicating the whole holiday to it, consider a multi-sports package (see next chapter). The whooshing can come later.

For those families for whom mere mountain biking somehow just isn't satisfying enough there's the new sport of cycling when you can't see where you're going. Yes, you go out at night and you do it on perilous paths and tracks. The organisers insist that modern lighting technology based on LEDs makes the experience safe and brings you closer to wildlife. Trees especially. **www.trailbreak.co.uk** Tel: 0118 976 2491.

## FURTHER INFORMATION

The Cyclists Touring Club is a good place to start (**www.ctc.org.uk** Tel: 0870 873 0060) while for mountain biking the specialist body is the International Mountain Biking Association (**www.imba.com**). Other useful sites include **www.trailquest.co.uk**, **www.nwmba.demon.co.uk** (for Wales) and **www.hmba.org.uk** (for the Highlands). For tour operators put 'cycling holidays' or 'mountain bike holidays' into your search engine together with the name of your chosen destination.

### Some specialist road bike operators

**www.cycling-for-softies.co.uk** Tel: 0161 248 8282

**www.bicyclebeano.co.uk** Tel: 01982 560 471

**www.wideopenroad.co.uk** Tel: 0797 457 2629

**www.lifecycleadventures.com** Tel: 0800 587 8663

**www.capital-sport.co.uk** Tel: 01296 631 671

### Some specialist mountain bike operators

**www.alpineelements.co.uk** Tel: 0870 011 1360

**www.trailbreak.co.uk** Tel: 0118 976 2491

**www.skedaddle.co.uk** Tel: 0191 265 1110

**www.roughtracks.com** Tel: 0700 056 0749

**www.cycleactive.co.uk** Tel: 01768 840 400

**www.outbreak-adventure.com** Booking online

## Some questions to ask

✓ Is this a suitable area for families?

✓ Are the roads quiet?

✓ What quality of bike are you supplying?

✓ What happens if there's a breakdown or a puncture?

✓ Do you have a back-up vehicle?

✓ Is bike hire included in the price or extra?

✓ Are new parts for wear and tear included in the rental price?

✓ Can we bring our own bikes?

✓ Is insurance included?

✓ (Mountain bikes only): Will it have suspension? In the front? In the rear?

## Why is this good for families?

Given today's traffic, only the quietest roads can be said to be suitable for families. Tracks are safer but harder work so you all need to be fairly fit. That having been said, it's more enjoyable away from the traffic and you can make it as easy or as hard as you like. You can stop when you want, divert if you like, and on one centre holidays decide on a day off if you need.

### Pros

● You'll get fit.

● You can cover a lot more ground than hiking.

### Cons

● Harder work than sunbathing on the beach.

● Cyclists are a little vulnerable on mountain tracks, and *extremely* vulnerable on busy roads.

## Where to go

On a road bike anywhere without traffic, especially the Cotswolds, Highlands and Islands, Ireland, rural France, inland Spain and California's wine country. On a mountain bike the Lake District, Pennines, Quantocks, Brecon Beacons, Snowdonia and Scottish Highlands in the UK; the Alps, Jura, Cevennes and Pyrenees in France; the Picos de Europa, Pyrenees, Sierra de Gredos and Sierra Nevada in Spain; Sardinia; Marin County, Lake Tahoe's Rim Trail, Mammoth Mountain and Santa Cruz in California.

## When

For road bikes, spring and autumn are best when the weather isn't too hot and places aren't too busy. For mountain bikes choose autumn (because there can still be snow on high ground in the spring).

## Price guide

*Road bikes:* A week's gastronomic bike tour in Provence or the Luberon with *Cycling For Softies* costs over £1,000 in high season, excluding flights, but companies that put less emphasis on luxury have holidays for half that.

*Mountain bikes:* A week's holiday in the Alps will cost from £350–£500 in basic accommodation, excluding flights. On top of that you'll have to pay from £70 up to more than £200 for the hire of a serious bike. For California you could pay as much as £2,000 for a 14 day mountain biking holiday. Most multi-activity tour companies include cycling and mountain biking.

# Unusual Family Holiday No. 27: Climbing

Climbing just isn't as popular a sport as it ought to be. Some instructors were wondering why. It occurred to them that it might have something to do with the fear of falling off and dying. So they determined to create an absolutely foolproof way for beginners – children as well as adults – to scale a rock face. And so the *via ferrata* was born. Essentially a *via ferrata* is a climbing route on which all the hardware is permanently installed (so there's no need to carry ropes and pitons and all of that). What's more, you can't fall off even if you want to because you're all clipped onto a steel cable. Which means you no longer have to worry about the kids getting hurt – nor you yourself.

Every mountain is different so every *via ferrata* has to be different, too. But, normally, in addition to the standard climbing 'pitches' there are also fun elements like rope bridges and ladders. If you've ever thought that climbing could be for your family, instruction at a *via ferrata* could be the best way to start. There are over 75 *via ferrata* in France (including half a dozen within easy reach of the Mediterranean coast), almost as many in Italy, 14 in Switzerland and four in Andorra (**www.viaferrata.org**).

Another way of getting started is an *indoor* climbing wall. It saves you having to travel all the way to a mountain and, what's more, it never rains. In America, indoor climbing is so popular it could almost be called a craze. But even Britain now has well over 250 walls, including flat places like Guildford where Craggy Island has a 10m wall. Indoor climbing has lots of advantages. It's far cheaper and somewhat safer than climbing mountains, it's accessible and, above all, its cool. You might never persuade your children to don plus fours and heavy boots but they'll be queuing up for the sort of kit that goes with this. To become a family of 'wall rats' contact the British Mountaineering Council (**www.thebmc.co.uk/indoor/walls/wall.asp** Tel: 0870 010 4878); for the world try **www.indoorclimbing.com**.

Specialists include **www.keswickclimbingwall.co.uk** Tel: 01768 772 000 and **www.indoorclimbingwalls.co.uk** Tel: 01443 710 749.

But if you insist on doing things the old fashioned way then Plas y Brenin, based in Snowdonia, has a special Introduction to Rock Climbing for Families **www.pyb.co.uk** Tel: 01690 720 214. From there, you can graduate to the Alps. Even Mont Blanc, western Europe's highest peak at 4,807m, is accessible to a family of adults and determined teenagers (**www.guides-mont-blanc.com** or **www. guides-du-montblanc.com**). If you'd also like to bag the highest mountain in the lower 48 states of the USA then that's Mt Whitney, a slightly easier proposition than Mont Blanc and 387m lower **www.nps.gov/seki/whitney.htm**.

Once you've climbed up something there's then the problem of getting down again. Usually there's an easy way round the back, but the smart solution is abseiling – sliding down a rope. Some people like it so much it's become an activity in its own right. The hard parts (if you don't have much of a head for heights) are hanging around for your turn and, when your turn comes, going over the edge. That's where the character building comes in because the descent itself – controlled by a simple friction device – is really very easy. So this is for children just as much as adults.

## FURTHER INFORMATION

Put 'climbing holiday' into your search engine together with the name of your chosen destination. For general information about climbing take a look at **www.abc-of-rockclimbing.com**. For the UK see **www.ukclimbing.com**. For information about Mont Blanc see **www.chamonix.net**. Exodus can take you around Mont Blanc and Mt Whitney but not to the summits (**www.exodus.co.uk** Tel: 0870 240 5550).

### Some specialist operators

**www.craggy-island.com** Tel: 01483 566 880

**www.activitywales.com** Tel: 01437 765 777

**www.blackmountain.co.uk** Tel: 01497 847 897

**www.rockandice.net** Tel: 01335 344 982

**www.wild-wales.co.uk** Tel: 01492 582 448

**www.rockandsun.com** Tel: 0871 871 6782

**www.action-outdoors.co.uk** Tel: 00 45 845 890 0362

**www.colletts.co.uk** Tel: 01763 289 660

**www.minster-alpine.co.uk** Tel: 0161 969 5603

### Some questions to ask

✓ Is this suitable for children?

✓ What experience do we require?

✓ What qualifications do you have?

✓ What qualifications could we attain?

✓ What equipment do we need to bring?

✓ Will we be insured?

✓ What happens if we discover we're afraid of heights?

### Why is this good for families?

Most climbing is co-operative.

### Pros

• Teaches confidence, self-reliance, leadership and judgement.

## Cons

- Older members of the family may look ridiculous in 'wall-rat' leotards.

- Potentially dangerous.

### Where to go

In the UK: Scotland especially Skye, the Cairngorms, Ben Nevis and Glencoe; Wales, especially Snowdonia, the Gower and Pembrokeshire; the Lake District, Yorkshire, the Peak District, Avon Gorge, Dartmoor, Cornwall's sea cliffs, Harrison's Rocks near Tunbridge Wells. Ireland: Donegal, the cliffs at Fair Head and Sligo, the Mourne, Wicklow, Comeragh and Connemara Mountains. The Alps, especially the Mont Blanc massif and the Italian Dolomites. The Pyrenees. The Sierra Nevada in California including Mt Whitney and the Yosemite Valley.

### When

Usually summer, but there's ice climbing in winter and indoor climbing all year.

### Price guide

Entrance to Craggy Island's climbing wall at Guildford is £9.50 plus £5 to hire equipment. Think in terms of just under £100 a day on a climbing course, with travel, accommodation and food on top. A week's climbing holiday in Austria with Minster Travel costs from around £450–£650, depending on accommodation and meals. If you get hooked, it will cost around £300 to equip each family member with basic climbing equipment (harness, helmet, backpack, boots).

## Unusual Family Holiday No. 28: Ghost Hunting

How fast can a ghost run? We only ask because if a ghost can run very quickly then ghost hunting must qualify as a physical activity. Anyway, that's what we've decided.

Believe it or not, quite a lot of companies are offering to scare you witless in return for money. And there are perfectly respectable hotel managers willing to let you sleep with a monk in chains or even a headless countess. And not just in eccentric old England. There are ghosts all over the place.

## FURTHER INFORMATION

For obvious reasons this activity is not something for the very young, but it's a great way of cementing a hand holding bond between teenager and scared stiff parent. For a general overview of what's going on within the paranormal community and where see **http://paranormality.com** and **www.psychics.co.uk**. For mysterious holidays look at the links in **www.travel-quest.co.uk**. To do your own thing in a reputedly haunted hotel in the UK look at the directory **www.english-inns.co.uk**. For the USA try **http://gocalifornia.about.com/cs/hauntedplaces.htm**. Or book the haunted tour on board one of the best known ex-cruise liners in the world at **www.queenmary,com** Tel:00 1 562 435 3511.The normally very wholesome Knotts Berry Farm in California turns spooky around Halloween and becomes Knotts Scary Farm **www.knottsberryfarm.com**.

### Some specialist operators

**www.paranormaltours.com** Tel: 0871 288 4026

Earth Mysteries and Sacred Site Tours Tel: 01874 624 936

**www.hauntingbreaks.co.uk** Tel: 01686 420 301

**www.sfghosthunt.com** Tel: 00 1 415 922 5590

### Some questions to ask

✓ Will we be frightened?

✓ Can we change rooms if we are/are not?

✓ Is this suitable for children?

✓ Is there medical help close by?

✓ Is there a guide?

✓ Do we get our money back if nothing happens?

### Why is this good for families?

This is probably not a subject for the under 12s but everybody loves a good mystery, and teenagers, in particular, like to be scared. It's just another of the odds things about them.

### Pros

● Brings the whole family together (in terror).

### Cons

- Sleepless nights

### Where to go

There are haunted houses and hotels all over the UK and Ireland and, indeed, the world.

### When

Halloween.

### Price Guide

Think in terms of £200 for a packaged ghost searching weekend, exclusive of travel.

## And finally

Skydiving might not seem to be a suitable family activity but there is a way of experiencing the exhilaration without the risk – or expense. Airkix at Milton Keynes has a vertical wind tunnel generating a blast of 150 mph, quite enough to keep somebody airborne. A one hour introduction costs £39.99 each (£34.99 off peak) **www.airkix.co.uk** Tel: 0845 331 6549.

## And even more finally

If nothing else tickles your combined fancies why not try *weaselling*? Weaselling is (we quote) 'wriggling, scrambling and squirming like a weasel' as you enter an underground labyrinth of tunnels, voids and spaces under a jumble of boulders that have lain undisturbed since the ice age. Not as intense as caving and with lots of opportunities to come up for air, it's perfect for families **www.scotmountain.co.uk** Tel: 01479 831331.

# Chapter 7

# Family Activity Holidays (Part Two), Getting Wet

**Unusual family holidays in this chapter: white water rafting, canyoning, canoeing, sailing, narrow boating and much more.**

Water adds a whole extra dimension to outdoor activities. There are literally dozens of different ways of using the stuff and new ones get invented every day. Here we suggest some of the best for families. And for those of you who can't make up your minds between the wet and the dry, we finish off with some multi-sports holidays that give you a taste of everything.

## Unusual Family Holiday No. 29: White Water Rafting

Talk white water rafting and most people think, *ouch*, tough guy stuff. Well, it all depends on the river, the snow melt and the amount of rain. In the right circumstances this is great fun for all the family and infinitely superior to anything on offer in a waterpark. Sitting in specially reinforced inflatables, and wearing life jackets and protective gear, everybody takes a paddle and does their best to avoid the rocks. Depending on the operator and the river, you can go for an hour, a day or even several days. Where young children are concerned you definitely need the kind of *flat* water that's found, for example, on the River Tay in Perthshire or the American River in California. The really white rivers will have an age minimum of, perhaps, 16.

### FURTHER INFORMATION

For general information about rafting take a look at **www.ukrafting.co.uk**, **www.jojaffa.com** and **www.realadventure.com**. In the UK it's always worth checking with the Adventure Activities Licensing Authority

**www.aala.org** Tel: 01222 755 715 to know if a company has been accredited. For the USA see **www.raftingamerica.com**; for the 'classic' take a look at **www.raftingthegrandcanyon.com** which outlines the various options.

## Some specialist operators

**www.rafting.co.uk** Tel: 01887 829 706

**www.naelimits.co.uk** Tel: 01350 727 242

**www.jjraftcanoe.com** Tel: 01978 860 763

**www.americanwhitewater.com** Tel: 1 800 825 3205

**www.activitiesabroad.com** Tel: 01670 789 991

**www.tirolrafting.com** Tel: 00 43 52 668 8116

## Some questions to ask

✓ What's the minimum age or weight?

✓ What sort of craft do you use?

✓ What state will the river be in?

✓ What grade is this section? (Grade 3 and below is recommended for the under 15s.)

✓ Does everybody get a chance to paddle?

✓ What happens if a child is thrown out of the boat?

✓ Is there an emergency boat standing by?

✓ Are we insured?

## Why is this good for families?

Since it's the river that supplies the energy, everybody irrespective of skill or age gets to enjoy the same thrill.

## Pros

● Half-drowning together is a great way of cementing family ties.

## Cons

● Potentially dangerous.

### Where to go

In Austria good centres include Kaprun, Zell am See and Saalbach; in France Chamonix and Les Gets; in northern Italy, the Brenta River in the Veneto region; in Spain the Noguera Pallaresa in the Eastern Pyrenees; in the USA, the American River (South Fork), just east of Sacramento, California.

### When

Depends on the river, but usually spring (when the snow melts) or summer.

### Price guide

A half-day trip on a calm section of the River Tay will cost around £30 each, while a two hour real white water experience will be around £45. For a two day expedition in the USA expect to pay from about £150 per person, including tent accommodation and food but not travel.

## Unusual Family Holiday No. 30: Canyoning – Nature's Waterpark

No matter how much they enjoy the things there are to do in the mountains there are always times that kids miss the beach. Especially when it's hot. Well, a canyon is a beach and a waterpark all rolled into one. There may be (depending on the canyon) deep pools for swimming, waterfalls to jump off, natural water chutes to whoosh along and cliffs to abseil down. The right canyon will put a smile on the face of every sad sand boy.

Of course, no two canyons are the same. Some, like the Gubiés del Parrissal in Catalonia's Puertos de Beceite amount to a series of natural swimming pools quite suitable (in summer) for youngish children in swimming costumes. Others, like the Llech near Prades in the French Pyrenees, involve wetsuits and long abseils, are only suitable for fit teenagers and adults who know no fear, and require a guide. In any case, a guide can add considerably to the canyoning experience by knowing, for example, where it is and isn't safe to jump. If there's any doubt, get a guide.

**WARNING**
Take careful note of the weather forecast. You don't want to be caught out in a deep canyon in a storm. Rain can quickly transform an exhilarating stream into a terrifying – and deadly – wall of water.

## FURTHER INFORMATION

Local tourism offices can supply a list of licensed operators. In the UK look for the Adventure Activities Licensing Authority sticker **www.aala.org** Tel: 01222 755 715. The Youth Hostels Association **www.yha.org.uk** offers canyoning at some of its properties. Also see **www.adventuredirectory.com**, **www.pyrenees.co.uk**, **www.travel-quest.co.uk** and **www.familyfirst.fr**. For specialist Grand Canyon trips look at **www.thecanyon.com**.

### Some specialist operators

**www.exodus.co.uk** Tel: 0870 240 5550

**www.ideealp.fr** Tel:00 33 60 914 8124

**www.mat-et-eau.fr** Tel: 00 33 68 156 2156

**www.responsibletravel.com** Tel: 01273 600 030

**www.activitiesabroad.com** Tel: 01670 789 991

**www.guara-canyoning.com** Tel: 00 34 97 431 9084

### Some questions to ask

✓ What age do children have to be?

✓ What's the highest abseil?

✓ Has there been recent heavy rain or is rain forecast (which might make the canyon dangerous)?

✓ What qualifications do you have?

✓ Are we insured?

✓ What are the rescue arrangements should there be an accident?

✓ Is there much of a walk at the beginning or end of the canyon?

✓ Do we need wetsuits and helmets? If so, do you supply them?

### Why is this good for families?

The moments of tension while waiting for a jump, slide or abseil can be very bonding for a family. Plenty of excitement and laughs (especially if somebody loses their swimsuit after a jump).

### Pros

• A natural waterpark experience up a mountain.

## Cons

- By their very nature there's no way out of some canyons except at the far end — once you start you're committed.

## Where to go

For good canyoning you need limestone. Best places are the Cevennes and the Pyrénées Orientales in France; the Sierra de Guara in the Spanish Pyrenees. In the USA there's the Grand Canyon.

## When

Depends on the canyon because there has to be the right amount of water, but usually summer.

## Price Guide

A half-day canyoning experience will cost around £45 per person, including hire of wetsuit and helmet if necessary. Expect to pay around £400 for a week's canyoning in basic accommodation.

# Unusual Family Holiday No. 31: Paddling Your Own Canoe

The great advantage of a river over the sea, of course, is that it does most of the work for you. With just the occasional dip of a paddle to keep you on course, villages, castles, restaurants, ducks, weeping willows and gorges come gliding past. Some operators even organise your overnight stops for you. All you have to do is float along until you come to the next hotel. Where young biceps are concerned this tends to make canoeing a better bet than sea kayaking. The wonderful thing about river canoes is the sense of being part of the countryside. You make no noise, cause no pollution, see wildlife others miss and get to places larger craft just can't reach. Rivers come in two categories. Fast and foamy or placid and peaceful. Most holidaymakers with children opt for the latter.

## FURTHER INFORMATION

If you want to get a feel for canoeing take a look at **www.jojaffa.com**, which is inspirational. For general information on canoeing in the UK and abroad take a look at **http://playak.com**. It's a good idea to read one of the canoeing magazines such as Canoe Focus (**www.canoefocus.demon.co.uk**).

The British Canoe Union has details of navigable rivers and
courses in Britain (**www.bcu.org.uk** Tel: 0115 982 1100); Wales
**www.welsh-canoeing.org.uk** Tel: 01678 521 083; Scotland
**www.scot-canoe.org** Tel: 0131 317 7314; Northern Ireland
**www.cani.org.uk** Tel: 0870 240 5065. Look at **www.yha.org** for details
of hostels where canoeing is available. For Ireland contact the Inland
Waterways Association of Ireland **www.iwai.ie/rentals/rentacanoe.html**
or for paddle surfing **www.kayaksurfireland.com**. For France see
**www.canoe-france.com**. For links to operators everywhere try
**www.responsibletravel.com** and **www.travel-quest.co.uk**.

## Some specialist operators

**www.activitiesabroad.com** Tel: 01670 789 991

**http://adrenalinantics.com** Tel: 01654 713 961

**www.headwater.com** Tel: 01606 720 099

**www.mountainandwater.co.uk** Tel: 01873 831 825

**www.voyageurs.co.uk** Tel: 00 353 28 2563 1730

**www.pyrenean-activities.com** Tel 00 33 4 68 04 72 61 or 00 33
614 528 205

**www.ardecheguides.com** Tel: 00 33 4 753 70623

**www.canoeoutpost.com** Tel: 00 1 863 494 1215

**www.exodus.co.uk** Tel: 0870 240 5550

**www.resonsibletravel.com** Tel: 01273 600 030

## Some questions to ask

✓ What age do children need to be?

✓ Will we be on our own or part of a group?

✓ Will there be a safety boat?

✓ What happens if we get into difficulties?

✓ Will we be insured?

✓ What do we need to bring?

✓ Will there be places to buy provisions?

✓ How far each day?

## Why is this good for families?

Canoes can be singles, doubles or even large enough for the whole family together.

## Pros

- You become part of the environment and get to see scenery hidden from everyone else.
- No noisy engine.
- Healthy.

## Cons

- You're rather tied to the environs of the river for everything from shopping to nightlife.
- Younger family members may get tired/sore.

## Where to go

Britain: the Dart, Dee, Isla, Severn, Spey, Thames, Usk, Wye. France: the Ardèche, Cèze, Dordogne, Drôme, Gardon, Hérault, Orb, Petit Rhône, Sorgue, Tarn, Ariège and Vezère. Spain: the Noguera Pallaresa. Portugal: the Mino, Gállego and Carasa. Florida: the Everglades National Park, the Wacissa, Aucilla and Sopchoppy Rivers.

## When

Summer except for rivers like Spain's Noguera Pallaresa which only have enough water in the spring.

## Price guide

A weekend on a British river will cost from around £200 while for a week's canoeing in France expect to pay from £750–£1,000 including ferry crossing or flight, accommodation, breakfast and evening meal.

# Unusual Family Holiday No. 32: Messing About In Boats

There is nothing – absolutely nothing – half so much worth doing as simply messing about in boats, as Ratty told Mole in *The Wind in the Willows*. How right he was. And he might have added that nothing – absolutely nothing – is half so good for a family holiday.

Our preference is for sail boats rather than motors, because, for one thing, there's so much more to do than just steer. There are sails to be changed and sheets (ropes) to be pulled, not to mention decks to be swabbed. Which gives everybody a real sense of doing something useful. Even heroic. Of course, if your children are more into torpor then you can equally mess about in motor boats which tend to be more spacious, not to say faster. But, motor or sail, the thing you have to remember about small boats is that there's not a lot of space to get away from one another. Two weeks in constant close confinement with testy teenagers could be hard.

There are basically four ways of going about the whole thing: flotilla, sailing school, skippered and bareboat.

A *flotilla* is the way for you all to get your hands on a boat even if no one in the family has a qualification or much experience (although some flotilla companies do insist on a minimum of knowledge). All explanations will be given at the initial briefing and there'll be people on the lead boat to sort you out if you get into problems. Of course, you'll be expected to stick, more or less, with the group, anchoring together at midday and again in the evening. On the plus side, that gives everyone the chance to make friends.

A *sailing school* will be much more structured, with the emphasis on learning and getting a certificate. You may be sleeping on the boat or you could have accommodation ashore and make day cruises. Towards the end of your holiday you might be allowed to hire a school boat to sail on your own.

*Skippered* charter means you pay for a qualified person to take charge of the boat. Be clear about how much members of the family want to join in handling the boat and how much they just want to laze around. If the boat is large enough and you're rich enough you can have people take care of everything, including fixing meals.

*Bareboat* is the ultimate freedom. It means you charter a yacht just for your family and go where you please (within agreed limits). Obviously, no one is going to let you loose with an expensive boat unless you have the necessary experience. A lot of companies insist on a paper qualification but, for those anarchic old sea dogs who have never bothered with that kind of thing, some will make their own judgement based on a written summary of your exploits and an assessment on the boat (it's pretty obvious who knows which way up a sail goes and who doesn't).

## FURTHER INFORMATION

Try **www.charternet.com** and **www.uk250.co.uk** for links to
sailing holidays and charter companies. For the USA try
**www.allthevacations.com** and then enter 'Florida yacht charters' or whatever
else you want.

## Some specialist operators

*Flotilla*

**www.minotaurholidays.com** Tel: 01785 285 434

**www.realadventures.com** Tel: 00 1 617 738 4700

**www.fyly.gr** Tel: 00 30 210 985 8670

**www.sunsail.com** Tel: 0870 777 0313

*Bareboat*

**www.nauticsail.gr** Tel: 00 30 210 982 3029

**www.sunsail.com** Tel: 0870 777 0313

**www.floridayacht.com** Tel: 00 1 305 293 0800 (also a sailing school)

*Skippered*

**www.nauticsail.gr** Tel: 00 30 210 982 30 29

**www.waterfantaseas.com** Tel: 00 1 305 531 1480 (Miami) or 00 1
954 524 1234 (Fort Lauderdale)

**www.swfyachts.com** Tel: 00 1 239 656 1339

*Sailing Schools*

**www.boss-sail.co.uk** Tel: 023 804 57733

**www.butesail.clara.net** Tel: 01700 504 881

**www.celticventures.com** Tel: 00 353 402 39418

**www.brittanysail.co.uk** Tel: 00 33 29 817 0131

**www.canarysail.com** Tel: 01438 880 890

**www.euro-sail.co.uk** Tel: 01473 833 001

**www.blunosa.it** Tel: 00 39 080 553 8808

**www.sunsail.com** Tel: 0870 770 6312

**www.seafarercruises.com** Tel: 0870 442 2447

**www.centurionyachting.co.uk** Tel: 0797 491 5944

## Some questions to ask

✓ How old do children need to be?

✓ What sailing experience do we need?

✓ Does the skipper need a paper qualification?

✓ Are you approved by the Royal Yachting Association?

✓ Do we have to stay with the flotilla all the time?

✓ How many hours sailing each day?

✓ What do we need to bring?

✓ Do we have to buy our own food?

✓ Who pays if, for example, a sail is damaged by the wind?

✓ What happens if someone is sick or injured?

✓ Will we be insured?

## Why is this good for families?

A boat offers something for everybody, from sunbathing to playing the role of 'deck ape' to rustling up a gourmet dinner in the galley.

## Pros

- The holiday with everything — boating, swimming, snorkelling, sunbathing, exploring ashore... The list goes on.

## Cons

- Seasickness — though this usually wears off after three days at most.

- Being cramped together in a small space, especially if the weather is bad.

## Where to go

If you're thinking in terms of a flotilla you're limited to where they operate. The Ionian is ideal, with plenty of anchorages just a short distance apart. The Cyclades, too. For bareboat or skippered charter you have a lot more flexibility — in UK waters Cornwall, the Isles of Scilly and the Western Isles are the best; the south-west coast of Ireland; in the Med the Balearics, Corsica, Sardinia, the Tuscan Islands, Sicily and its islands. South-west Florida, including the Florida Keys, is one of the top charter destinations in the world, a mass of islands and inlets with unrivalled facilities.

## When

We've had some great sailing in the Med – and even in Britain – in the winter but the whole experience is generally much more enjoyable from May to October (but excepting overcrowded August). In the Florida Keys May can be good – June to November is hurricane season and November to April is high season.

## Price guide

Flotilla holidays cost from around £400 up to about £1,500 per person for two weeks, including flights, depending on season and how many are sharing a boat. Bareboat charter is about the same and you'll also need to leave a security deposit of from a few hundred up to maybe £2,000, depending on the value of the boat. Fuel, port fees and food will be on top. A skipper will cost around £1,000 a week. At the top end, for a large yacht with skipper and crew to take care of everything the sky is the limit – or, should we say, the ocean.

# Unusual Family Holiday No. 33: On The Cut

If you don't think your family – or you yourself – are quite ready for waves then something inland might be better.

For those who aren't familiar with it the canal system in Britain can come as a very pleasant surprise. Known to the cognoscenti as 'the cut' and for the most part hidden away from 'ordinary' people, some 2,000 miles of waterways criss-cross the country as if in a parallel world. There's a very relaxing speed limit of 4mph – to protect the banks from wash – but, in reality, you probably won't average more than 3mph which means that anyone who wants to stretch their legs can easily keep up. And when it comes to time to stop for the day you can tie up more or less anywhere on the towpath side (taking care not to obstruct a lock). There are no parking meters here.

Puttering along on water in the heart of the countryside with sheep and cows on either side is pleasantly bizarre. But quite a lot of enthusiasts adore the industrial landscapes just as much, especially if they're derelict. And just about everybody loves to find that special little pub by the lock gates, with a garden for youngsters.

Ah, yes, the locks. After the novelty has worn off, people end up either relishing them or hating them. For the former, the British canal system provides some formidable challenges – Delph, Bratch, Caen Hill, the Rothersthorpe Flight, the Wolverhampton 21. But once the kids are honed into an effective fighting force you'll be through them like an otter in a drainpipe.

The traditional canal boat is, of course, the narrow boat, so called because British canals are, well, narrow and so the boats had to be as well. You can also hire small motor cruisers but, somehow, they're just not right. They go *wah-ah-aah* whilst a narrow boat makes a nice, con-templative *chug-chug-chug*. Real narrow boats are huge affairs stretching on, it seems, for miles. You'll probably hire something mod-ern and shorter that sleeps four or, for a bigger family, eight.

Continental waterways, on the other hand, aren't narrow at all. Some of them, in fact, are quite frighteningly wide with significant currents. Well, the Continent is just so much *bigger*. So a narrow boat wouldn't be much good there. On the Continent motorboats that go *wah-ah-aah* are positively ideal.

## FURTHER INFORMATION

You can find out almost everything you need to know from the links on **www.canals.com**. Also take a look at **www.britishwaterways.co.uk** and **www.waterscape.com**. For a one stop check on the availability of boats from some 30 companies go to **www.waterwaysholidays.com** (Tel: 0870 747 2934); **www.europeafloat.com** has an index of hire companies. If you like the idea of inland waterways but don't want canals take a look at **www.norfolkbroads.com**.

### Some inland waterways companies

**www.viking-afloat.com** Tel: 01905 610 660

**www.napton-marina.co.uk** Tel: 01926 813 644

**www.kateboats.co.uk** Tel: 01926 492 968

**www.ashbyboats.co.uk** Tel: 01455 212 671

**www.waterwaysholidays.com** Tel: 0870 747 2934 (UK, Ireland and France)

**www.blakes.co.uk** Tel: 0870 220 2498 (UK & France)

**www.crownblueline.com** Tel: 0870 160 5634 (UK, France, Germany, Holland, Italy)

**www.swrecreation.com** (California)

## Some questions to ask

✓ What age do children have to be?

✓ Is the canal in a good state of repair? (Many aren't.)

✓ Is there enough water in the canal? (Some have sections which have become almost too shallow to navigate.)

✓ How many lock gates are there on this section of canal?

✓ Are there pubs with gardens for children?

✓ Is there any form of heating?

✓ Do we have to empty the toilets?

✓ Where can we buy provisions?

✓ Are there any things to do along the canal/river?

✓ Are there marinas we can put into?

✓ What happens if there's a problem with the boat?

✓ Will we be insured in case of a collision?

## Why is this good for families?

A canal holiday allows you not only to mess about in boats in a fairly safe environment but also to mess about in the countryside and even, if you feel like it, the town.

## Pros

- No seasickness.

- Plenty of tranquillity.

- About as reasonable a holiday as you can get.

## Cons

- Working the locks is pretty hard work.

- It can all get a bit grubby.

## Where to go

In Britain the Llangollen Canal has everything to satisfy the unconvinced while the Caldon, especially the Consall Forge section, is by general consent one of the most beautiful canals in the country. Other good bets are the Southern Oxford, the Grand Union, the Staffs and Worcester, Titford, the Leeds and

Liverpool, Rochdale, and, in Scotland, the Forth and Clyde canals. For motor boating on inland waterways abroad try the Shannon and Erne in Ireland; the Muritz Lake region of northern Germany; and in France, Alsace-Lorraine, the Garonne in Aquitaine, the 400 miles of waterways in Brittany, the Camargue (for white horses, black bulls and pink flamingos), the Lot (gorges), the Loire/Nivernais (chateaux) and the Canal du Midi. Florida is a paradise for inland waterways; in California go to Shasta Lake which is set in a wilderness of half a million acres.

### When

Most European operators open for business in May and run through to October. Florida's summer hurricane season may be worth risking on dry land but less so on water. California's Shasta Lake is not for the winter.

### Price guide

A narrow boat for a family of four costs from around £500 up to £1,000 a week and for eight from around £750 up to £1,500, so reckon on £100–£200 a head if the boat is full. Motor boats are similar but the truly luxurious can cost much more. Shasta Lake, California will cost from around £1,000 a week for a houseboat for 10 in spring/autumn up to as much as £4,000 a week for a houseboat sleeping 20 in summer. In all cases travel and food will be on top.

## Unusual Family Holiday No. 34: Multi-Sports

A holiday devoted to, say, canoeing or riding is all very well if you're an enthusiast. But a lot of active families prefer a little variety. In other words, not day after day of climbing but *one* day of climbing followed by *one* day of mountain biking and *one* day of rafting, and so on. Not to mention a day of sightseeing and a day of doing nothing. There are three basic ways of going about it. Firstly, you can stay at a specialist centre where lots of different activities are on offer (but the accommodation is usually basic). Normally, you can elect to do everything together as a family or let the kids go to special activities for youngsters – some centres even have women only activities. When you meet in the evenings or at meal times you'll always have plenty to talk about. Secondly, you can stay in a hotel from which your tour operator takes you to a different activity each day. Or, thirdly, you can go independently and buy your activities one at a time.

In the Ardèche region of France, Acorn Adventure Holidays is an example of the first category. Accommodation is in tents ready pitched in semi-circles to enhance community spirit, and activities include canoeing and rock climbing. Exodus Travel, normally associated with grown-up serious adventure stuff, has family holidays in the second category, embracing hiking, rock climbing, canyoning, mountain biking, riding, caving and canoeing.

Not all activity holidays are out in the wilds. PGL's Chateau de Grand Romaine centre is just 20 miles from the centre of Paris – close enough to accommodate a day trip to the Eiffel Tower and only a 20 minute drive from Disneyland Resort Paris (if you have any energy left over). Here you can try archery, abseiling, climbing, the high trapeze, mountain biking, orienteering or the dreaded zip wire. Parents be warned: you'll be encouraged to be the first down it – or onto the disco floor.

If you prefer watersports, Sunsail has something for just about everyone, including windsurfing, dinghy sailing, waterskiing, yachts and motor boats. Non-sailors can enjoy swimming pools, tennis courts, fitness centres and, of course, the beach or join the children's clubs (Snappers 2-4 years, Sea Urchins 5-7, Gybers 8-12 and Beach Team 13-16) for everything from treasure hunts to junior discos. At Empuriabrava on the Costa Brava (a world famous skydiving centre) Activities Abroad has an even more eclectic programme including orienteering, abseiling, zip wire descents and exploring caves and creeks in sea kayaks.

For something completely different why not try a bush craft and wilderness course? At the Woodcraft School in far flung West Sussex you'll learn how to make camp fires, find and purify water, track and identify wildlife and all those things you've seen Ray Mears do on the telly.

## FURTHER INFORMATION

### Some specialist operators

**www.activitiesabroad.com** Tel: 01670 789 991

**www.sunsail.com** Tel: 0800 652 6520

**www.exodus.co.uk** Tel: 0870 240 5550

**www.adventurecompany.co.uk** Tel: 0845 450 5311

**www.explore.co.uk** Tel: 0870 333 4001

**www.activealpine.com** Tel: 020 7692 0939

**www.guerba.co.uk** Tel:01373 826 611

**www.alpactive.com** Tel: 0845 120 9872

**www.peakretreats.co.uk** Tel: 0870 770 0408

**www.espritholidays.co.uk** Tel: 01252 618 300

**www.clubmed.com** Tel: 0845 367 6767

**www.keycamp.co.uk** Tel: 0870 700 0750

**www.trekamerica.co.uk**. Tel: 0870 444 8735

**www.eurocamp.co.uk** Tel: 0870 366 7552

**www.canvasholidays.co.uk** Tel: 0870 192 1159

**www.pgl.co.uk** Tel: 0870 050 7507

**www.woodcraftschool.co.uk** Tel: 01730 816 299

**www.acornadventure.com** Tel: 0800 074 9791

**www.footloose.com** Tel: 00 1 973 983 1144

## Some questions to ask

✓ What ages are these activities suitable for?

✓ Are there dangers?

✓ What qualifications do you have?

✓ Will we take part in activities as a family group?

✓ Are we insured?

✓ Are all activities covered in the price or do we pay separately for each one?

✓ Is sleeping in dormitories or private rooms?

✓ What non-active things are there to do?

## Why is this good for families?

Something for every age and taste (as long as it's active).

## Pros

• It's the ideal way of trying out a whole range of different sports.

## Cons

- Accommodation is often rather basic.

## Where to go

Scotland, Wales, the Alps, the Pyrenees, California.

## When

Spring and autumn for the really energetic stuff. Summer or autumn for anything involving water.

## Price guide

Think around £500 minimum per person for a week all inclusive, including a basic package of activities. A family of four can expect to pay about £400 for a three day woodcraft course in West Sussex; around £1,400 for seven days on a PGL Family Active holiday using own transport or £1,700 by coach; around £3,500 for seven days at Sunsail's base at Vounaki, Greece — with special courses costing around £65 to £100 extra.

---

# And finally

If your family can't decide between a holiday climbing in the mountains and a holiday at the beach then coasteering could be for you. A fairly new sport, it involves working your way along a rugged stretch of coast by whatever means necessary. Sometimes you'll be traversing cliff faces on ledges, sometimes you'll be abseiling down cliffs, sometimes you'll be jumping and sometimes you'll just be swimming. Penhale, near Newquay in Cornwall, is one place you can give it a go. A half-day trip costs about £40, including the hire of a wetsuit, helmet and buoyancy aid **www.penhaleadventure.com** Tel: 0800 781 6861.

# Chapter 8

# Cultural Holidays

**Unusual family holidays in this chapter: literary walks, music festivals and much more.**

Nowadays, culture – in the widest sense – is an important part of everybody's life. So why shouldn't it be an important part of your family holiday as well? The only problem might be in agreeing exactly what type of culture you're going in pursuit of. And when it comes to things like pop festivals, your kids are probably going to say they're embarrassed about having you around. (But that's really only because they're jealous that you can dance better than they can.)

## Unusual Family Holiday No. 35: Fact And Fiction

We were both great fans of Enid Blyton's Famous Five when we were growing up but, sadly, none of those adventures ever happened to us. Perhaps it was because we didn't know the right places to go. But we know now and we're going to tell you. Remember Kirrin Castle in *Five On A Treasure Island*? Well, that was based on Corfe Castle in Dorset. Corfe Castle, you might point out, isn't on an island. Well, no, but that, of course, was just a ruse to stop people finding the real treasure that's undoubtedly still there. And while your children are searching for it they might even come across the secret tunnels that are believed to link the castle with the nearby village.

Then there was Whispering Island which featured in *Five Have A Mystery To Solve*. It's real name is Brownsea Island in Poole Harbour and in Blyton's day it was privately owned. Landing was forbidden which, naturally, gave rise to all kinds of rumours, most of them no doubt true. Thanks to the National Trust you and your children can nowadays visit Brownsea Island but, despite the many who have visited, the mystery of what the reclusive owners had been up to has never been solved. Yet!

We could go on. But it would be better if you simply went along to The Ginger Pop Shop in Corfe Castle village and joined one of the guided tours run by its owner Viv Endecott.

Or perhaps you'd be more interested in meeting up with Winnie the Pooh? Poohsticks Bridge still exists at Hartfield, East Sussex and we've been there quite a few times but always missed him. You might be more lucky but, even if not, you can still play the venerable game of Poohsticks in which you all drop a stick into the water from one side of the bridge then race across to the other side to see whose comes out first. Quite possibly Pooh might be taking a stroll with Tigger and Piglet and the rest in Hundred Acre Wood, which, in reality, is in the adjacent Ashdown Forest.

Apart from anything else, there's quite a fascination in seeing how fact is transformed into fiction by the creative mind. Blyton wrote a staggering 700 books and could knock one off in a week. If you'd like to learn a little bit more about how it's done (and maybe even have a go) then you might like to visit the Roald Dahl Museum And Story Centre at Great Missenden, Buckinghamshire or the Seven Stories Centre for Childrens' Books in Newcastle upon Tyne.

## FURTHER INFORMATION

**www.gingerpop.co.uk** Tel: 01202 620 660 – guided tours around Corfe Castle village and area by Viv Endecott whose Ginger Pop Shop sells books and toys from the 1940s/50s.

**www.sevenstories.org.uk** Tel: 0845 271 0777 – manuscripts and artwork from Britain's leading children's authors and illustrators.

**www.roalddahlmuseum.org** Tel: 01494 892 192 – learn how Roald Dahl lived, became inspired and wrote.

For details of the thousands of literary walking tours and similar all over the world try putting the name of your literary hero into your search engine together with the word 'tour' and the name of the destination. Here are a few suggestions:

**www.literarywalks.co.uk** Tel: 020 7686 4996 Walks include Coleridge & Highgate as well as Romantics In Hampstead.

**www.angelwalks.co.uk** Tel: 07796 673 846. Literary walks in East London.

**www.gardenvisit.com** Itineraries around London's parks, gardens and heaths.

**http://www3.hants.gov.uk** Details of literary itineraries in Hampshire. For Gilbert White and Jane Austen Tel: 01420 511270; for Charles Dickens Tel: 023 9282 6722

**www.visityork.org** Literary itineraries around York.

**www.rothaymanor.co.uk** Tel: 01539 433 605 A full five nights on the trail of writers, poets and artists in the Lake District.

**www.hfholidays.co.uk** Tel: 020 8905 9556 All kinds of themed walks from a specialist tour operator including Wuthering Heights, Beatrix Potter and Sherlock Holmes.

**http://gonyc.about.com** — links to dozens of walking tours in New York.

**www.centralpark.com** Walks in Central Park, New York.

## Some questions to ask

✓ Is this tour/museum suitable for children?

✓ What size is the group?

✓ How far will we walk?

✓ Will there be refreshments/meals?

✓ Will there be any special children's activities?

✓ What happens if it rains?

## Why is this good for families?

A good choice of subject — say, a long established children's author — spans the generations.

## Pros

● An insight into the creative process.

## Cons

● Young children may be bored with walking and talking.

## Where to go

There's hardly a place that didn't inspire some artist or writer.

## When

Usually the summer but could be any time.

## Price guide

You can pick up itineraries at tourist offices and set off on your own for free. Guided walks begin at as little as £5 but go up to £50 and more for a day. The five day tour of the Lake District based at the Rothay Manor (above) costs from £510.

# Unusual Family Holiday No. 36: Music And Arts Festivals

As the centrepiece of a family holiday some sort of cultural festival is a terrific idea. For a start, there's great entertainment every night and, in some cases, all day long, too. And if you choose the right location you can combine a festival with sightseeing and other activities, including the beach.

**Glastonbury** is about the largest festival in the world to be held in a field, or rather 900 acres of fields, in the Vale of Avalon (**www. glastonburyfestivals.co.uk** Tel: 0870 165 2005). But with all those tales of sex and drugs is it really suitable for children? And with all that mud is it really suitable for parents? The answer, surprisingly, is yes. (The main problem won't be getting the kids to agree to go but getting them to agree that *you* can go as well.) But it's not all pop groups, although you might all be very happy if it was. There's also jazz, theatre, circus and cabaret, including acts especially for children.

During the three days of the festival, usually at the end of June, the standard way of getting some sleep is to bring a tent. If you want a little more luxury there's a special area designated for caravans/camping cars. But the most luxurious accommodation on offer is Camp Kerala, run by a separate organisation and three minutes from Gate C. Fifty tents, about as luxurious as tents can be, are available. See **www. campkerala.com**.

*Nearest beach:* 30 minutes – you could also be in Weston-super-Mare in about 45 minutes and Minehead in one hour.

*Other things to see and do:* Bath, Bristol; hiking in the Mendip Hills.

**The Isle of Wight Festival** used to have the word 'Pop' in the title and was once the British answer to Woodstock (**www.isleofwightfestival.org** Tel: 0870 532 1321. June.) Things are a bit tamer now and there may never again be such a classic line up as Joni Mitchell, Miles Davis, Jimi Hendrix, Joan Baez and Leonard Cohen back in 1970. But it's all a lot more child friendly.

*Nearest beach:* It's a small island with beaches everywhere.

*Other things to see and do:* Carisbrooke Castle, Nunwell House and Osbourne House (Queen Victoria's family home).

**The Edinburgh International Festival** is the place to keep the whole family occupied night and day for anything up to three weeks. And it's all during the school holidays in August. Given the statistics there has to be more than enough for every different taste in the tribe – over 25,000 performances of something like 1,700 shows in a total of more than 200 venues embracing classical music, opera, dance, film, theatre, exhibitions, books, talks and gigs. It's been calculated that to see everything would take more than five years non-stop. The so called Fringe, started by a few disconsolate performers not invited to the main festival, is, if anything, more famous and includes all the anarchic stuff likely to appeal to teenagers. For general information see **www. edinburghfestivals.co.uk**. For tickets see **www.eif.co.uk** (Tel: 0131 473 2099) and **www.edfringe.com** (Tel: 0131 226 0026).

*Nearest beach:* Edinburgh is on the Firth of Forth but the best bet is probably North Berwick, about 40 minutes away.

*Other things to see and do:* National Gallery of Scotland, Scottish National Gallery of Modern Art, Palace of Holyroodhouse, the Castle.

**The Proms and Kids Week, London**. The Proms can make a great introduction to classical concert going. When the kids are standing on the floor of the Royal Albert Hall with a thousand other, mostly young, enthusiasts it's hard not to become infected. Promming places can be bought at the door from as little as a few pounds. The festival season of 70 or so concerts runs from mid-July until early September **www.bbc.co.uk/proms/** Tel: 020 7589 8212. Kids Week has been running for about 10 years now and, despite the title, usually covers the last two weeks in August. One part is nothing more than a free seat – a child between five and 16 can go free when accompanied by a full paying adult (and two more children can go half price). But far more exciting is that children can get involved in set design, script writing, costume workshops and even learn to perform. And there's even fun for the under fives **www.kidsweek.co.uk** Tel: 0870 400 0800.

*Nearest beach:* London now has its own beach in front of the Royal Festival Hall. Or you can do what generations of Londoners used to do before cheap airlines and take the train to Southend-on-Sea.

*Other things to see and do:* Take a look at Chapter 2.

**Rock in Rio** is actually in Lisbon, Portugal. The name indicates the kind of exotic experience it is, with past acts including Santana, Jamiroquai, Shakira and Sting. Lisbon's first Rock in Rio was only in 2005 but it seems set to continue. End May/June (**www.rockinrio-lisboa.sapo.pt**).

*Nearest beach:* Lisbon is near the mouth of the Rio Tejo but it's best to get well clear of the pollution by taking the train at least as far as Carcavelos, Parede, Estoril or Cascais on the north side of the estuary or, on the south side, you'll find the Costa da Caparica to be a thoroughly Portuguese experience.

*Other things to see and do:* The art collection in the Museu Gulbenkian which includes works by Degas, Manet, Monet, Renoir and Turner. The summer residence of the kings of Portugal at nearby Sintra.

**Nice Jazz.** That's Nice to rhyme with peace, not nice to rhyme with rice. If your youngsters are into jazz (but towards the rock end) then Cimiez Park in the well known Côte d'Azur resort is the place to be in July. Past acts have included Randy Newman and Suzanne Vega **www.nicejazzfest.com**.

*Nearest beach:* it's just a couple of kilometres to the famous Promenade des Anglais.

*Other things to see and do:* Don't miss the Matisse in the Villa des Arènes, or Chagall's Biblical Message or Rodin, Degas, Dufy, Monet and Sisley in the Beaux Arts.

**The Peralada Festival** held in the open air in the grounds of a castle in Spain in July/August combines a magical location with a mostly classical repertoire. If your children are old enough to stay up that late you can round off with dinner in the gardens **www.festivalperalada.com** Tel: 00 34 93 503 8646.

*Nearest beach:* The Costa Brava resorts of Roses and Llança are just 10 minutes away by car.

*Other things to see and do:* Salvador Dalí's house in Port Lligat and his theatre museum in Figueres; the Greco-Roman ruins at Empúries; the Garrotxa volcanic zone.

**The Verona Opera Festival** might be more popular with the kids than you imagine, given that opera now accompanies all kinds of sporting events. The setting in the 1st Century CE Roman amphitheatre, where gladiatorial contests once took place, is a spectacle in itself. Mid-June to end-August **www.arena.it** Tel: 00 39 045 800 5151.

*Nearest beach:* You could be swimming at Sirmione's Lido on Lake Garda within half an hour by car.

*Other things to see and do:* The Scaliger tombs, the Castelvecchio, the Basilica di San Zeno Maggiore, the Teatro Romano.

## FURTHER INFORMATION

For festivals in Britain see **www.artsfestivals.co.uk**. Local councils are often involved in festivals; for their websites see **www.direct.gov.uk**. For jazz see **www.jazzservices.org.uk**. For folk festivals see **www.folkandroots.co.uk**. For the USA take a look at **www.festivalfinder.com**; for country music festivals in the USA see **www.netunes.com/country-festivals.htm** or **http://countrymusic.about.com**.

For links to major festivals all over the world see **www.somusical.com** and **www.festivals.com**. For festivals of 'world' music see **www.womad.org**. For details of music competitions all over the world contact the World Federation Of International Music Competitions (**www.wfimc.org** Tel: 00 42 23 21 36 20).

### Some other music and arts festivals

#### Britain

**www.cambridgefolkfestival.co.uk** Tel: 01223 357 851 Cambridge Folk Festival. Late July.

**www.hayfestival.com** Tel: 0870 990 1299 Meet your favourite author in Hay, a crazy village in the Black Mountains of Wales with only 1,300 inhabitants but 39 bookshops. Ten days from late May until early June.

**www.breconjazz.co.uk** Tel: 01874 611 622 Brecon Jazz Festival. August. Britain's top jazz festival

**www.dokeswick.com** Tel: 01900 602 122 Keswick Jazz Festival. May. Over 100 jazz events.

**www.cheltenhamfestivals.co.uk** Tel: 01242 262 626 Classical music, jazz, folk and literature.

**www.bathfestivals.org.uk** Tel: 01225 462 231 Music and literature.

**www.aldeburgh.co.uk** Tel: 01728 687 110 Classical music, jazz and carnival.

**www.chifest.org.uk**. Tel: 01243 781 312. Chichester Festival. 200 events. July.

**www.buxtonfestival.co.uk** Tel: 01298 72289. Buxton Opera Festival. July. In the restored Edwardian Buxton Opera House.

**www.gs-festival.co.uk**. Tel: 01422 323 252. Buxton's Gilbert & Sullivan Festival. August.

**www.thetwomoorsfestival.com**. Tel: 01643 831 006. Two Moors Festival. Mid-October. Exmoor/Dartmoor.

## France

**www.festival-aix.com** Tel: 00 33 4 42 17 34 00. Aix-en-Provence. June/July.

**www.suds-arles.com** Tel: 00 33 4 90 96 06 27. Arles Festival Des Musiques Du Monde. Mid-July. Over 500 concerts of music from all over the world.

**www.prades-festival-casals.com**. Tel: 00 33 4 68 96 33 07. Prades Festival. Late July to mid-August. Chamber music festival begun by cellist Pablo Casals in 1950.

**www.circonautes.com** Tel: 00 33 1 40 680 772. International Circus Festival of Tomorrow. January.

## Belgium

**www.amisduclavecin.be** Tel: 00 32 016 480 836. Harpsichord festival in Brabant. Spring.

## Netherlands

**www.grachtenfestival.nl** Tel: 00 31 20 421 4542. Classical music on and beside Amsterdam's canals. August.

## Spain

**www.festivalsantander.com** Tel: 00 34 942 210 508. Santander Festival Internacional. All August. Music, dance and theatre in the Palacio de Festivales.

**www.granadafestival.org** Tel: 00 34 958 221 844. Granada Festival Internacional de Musica y Danza. End-June to early July. Includes some 60 performances in the Alhambra, one of the most beautiful buildings in the world.

## Portugal

**www.estorilfestival.net** 00 351 214 685 199 July/August.

## Italy

**www.newoperafestivaldiroma.com** Tel: 00 39 340 088 00 77 Rome New Opera Festival. In the courtyard of the Basilica of San Clemente.

## Austria

**www.salzburgfestival.at** Tel: 00 43 662 804 55 00 Late July to end-August.

**www.schubertiade.at** Tel: 00 43 557 672 091 Schubertiade. Mostly in Schwarzenberg, May to August. Europe's leading chamber music festival.

## Germany

**www.bayreuther-festspiele.de** Bayreuth. July/August.

**www.beethovenfest.de** Tel: 00 49 0180 500 1812. Bonn. September/October.

## Greece

**www.greekfestival.gr** Tel: 00 30 210 928 2900 The Athens Festival (May-October), the Epidaurus Festival of classical drama (July/August), the Patra Festival (July-September) and much more.

## USA

**www.musicfestivalofthehamptons.com** Tel: 00 1 800 644 4418 New York. July.

**www.nycstreetfairs.com** Tel: 00 1 212 809 4900 Music throughout the year on the streets of New York.

**www.filmlinc.com** Tel: 00 1 212 875 5050 New York Film Festival. September/October.

**www.coconutgroveartsfest.com** Tel: 00 1 305 447 0401 February. Florida.

**www.hollywoodbowl.com** Tel: 00 1 213 850 2000 Classical music, jazz and pop. June to September. California.

**www.montereyjazzfestival.com** Tel: 00 1 408 649 1770 World's oldest continuously running jazz festival. April. California.

**www.roguefestival.com** Tel: 00 1 5597 091 464 Fresno. March. California.

**www.harmonyfestival.com** Tel: 00 1 707 861 2035. Santa Rosa. June. Outdoor music with environmentalism. California.

**www.bachfestival.org** Tel: 00 1 408 624 2046. Bach festival in Carmel, California. July/August.

## Some specialist operators

**www.travelforthearts.co.uk** Tel: 020 8799 8350

**www.chambermusicholidays.co.uk** Tel: 01202 528 328

**www.martinrandall.com** Tel: 020 8742 3355

**www.archersdirect.co.uk** Tel: 0870 460 3894

**www.hfholidays.co.uk** Tel: 020 8905 9556

## Some questions to ask

✓ Is this event suitable for children?

✓ Are all concerts included in the price or are some extra?

✓ What category are the seats?

✓ Will we have a good view?

✓ Are any daytime activities included?

✓ Is transport to the concert venue included?

✓ What other things are there to do in the area?

✓ What happens if it rains?

## Why is this good for families?

A festival gives a real focus to a holiday – provided you all like the same music.

## Pros

- The family that bops together, stops together.

Live performances of classical music can sometimes inspire youngsters where CDs fail – especially if other young people are there.

## Cons

- A child fidgeting, talking or, worse, crying, through Barber's Adagio is embarrassing, to say the least.

- Some festivals provide nothing to do in the daytime.

- Mud (usually only applies to outdoor festivals).

## Where to go

The list is growing all the time and many of the smaller events are more enjoyable than the famous ones.

## When

Most festivals are in the summer.

## Price guide

You can camp at one of the smaller pop festivals and spend no more than £200 as a family for a weekend, including food and your pitch. The big pop events aren't cheap but they're good value when you consider the enormous number of acts you get to see and hear. For a weekend think in terms of around £60 a head just for admission while the week long concerts might be double that. At the top end of the scale, prices of £2,000–£3,000 each are not unusual for a fully inclusive week at a European festival of classical music and opera, but with budget airlines and hotels you can make your own arrangements much more cheaply.

---

## And finally

How about a very cultured coach tour of Bavarian castles? No, no, not a motor coach. We're talking about a *real* coach. A horse drawn coach. Granted it tends to cost a little more than the modern version but it's an experience you and the kids will never forget. With *Coaching In Bavaria* you'll cover 18 to 35 miles a day and clip clop up to 'mad' King Ludwig's Neuschwanstein, the ultimate fairy tale castle, as well as the palace of Hohenschwangau. A two day tour costs from around £250 each while for two weeks (in Hungary) you'll pay around £3,600 each. Oh, and you need to be good at waving. **www.intetra.net** Tel: 00 49 880 8386.

# Chapter 9

# Educational Holidays

**Unusual family holidays in this chapter: learning a foreign language, photography, painting, history, all about volcanoes, and much more.**

They say travel broadens the mind. Which should make any holiday an educational experience. Yet researchers have recently discovered that two weeks of doing nothing very much can actually lower IQ by up to a staggering 20 points. The moral is clear. Take the family on holiday by all means, but make sure it includes plenty of intellectual stimulation.

## Unusual Family Holiday No. 37: Learn The Language

Learning the language is the most obvious way you can all add to your accomplishments whilst abroad. Study a language course on CD-ROM before you go and arm every member of the family with a pocket phrase book. It's also a great idea to watch a DVD that's in both English and the language you want to learn. The kids' favourite film or TV series is ideal. Just keep running it and running it until you can all repeat some of the 'catch phrases'. But if you really want to make some progress then book a language course. Cactus Language, for example, runs special programmes for families to learn Spanish, French, Italian and German in the countries. Lessons are usually in the mornings leaving the afternoons free for normal holiday activities **www.cactuslanguage.com** Tel: 0845 139 4775. Others combine two subjects, such as Spanish with everything flamenco (**www.carmencuevas .com** Tel: 00 34 958 22 10 62). Finally, if you can all stay with a local family that speaks no English you'll not only get plenty of free practice but you'll learn all those colloquial expressions the language school never mentioned.

## FURTHER INFORMATION

Put 'language school' into your search engine, together with the name of the destination. At **www.abroadlanguages.com** you'll find details of and links to a wide variety of language schools.

### Some specialist operators

**www.cesalanguages.com** Tel: 01209 211 800

**www.euroacademy.co.uk** Tel: 020 8297 0505

**www.elemadrid.com** Tel: 00 34 65 685 1635

**www.abanico-es.com** Tel: 00 34 952 20 61 82

**www.accord-langues.com** Tel: 00 33 1 55 33 52 33

**www.scuolaleonardo.com** Tel: 00 39 55 26 11 81

**www.coeurdefrance.com** Tel: 00 33 24 879 3408

**www.caledonialanguages.co.uk** Tel: 0131 621 7721

**www.hispalense.com** Tel: 00 34 956 680 927 (Tarifa)

**www.institutobabel.com** Tel:00 34 958 272 529 (Granada)

**www.alpha.at** Tel: 00 43 1503 6969 (learn German in Austria)

**www.donquijote.org** Tel: 00 34 923 268 860 or 00 34 923 277 200

### Some questions to ask

✓ Will we have our lessons together?

✓ Will we be with other families?

✓ What is the usual class size?

✓ How many hours of lessons per day?

✓ Can you arrange accommodation?

✓ What other things are there to do in the area?

✓ Will we get some kind of certification at the end?

### Why is this good for families?

A great way to help the kids with their language classes at school and a useful skill for adults, too.

### Pros

- Total holiday immersion is the fastest way for the kids and you to progress.

### Cons

- Expensive compared with evening classes at home or self-teaching methods such as cassettes and DVDs.

### Where to go

Capital cities are best for avoiding regional accents and dialects, but beach resorts provide a better reward for the kids' efforts.

### When

If language is the only consideration choose the low season.

### Price guide

Three hours of classes per day spread over two weeks cost around £200. Private lessons cost around £20 an hour. Language schools don't normally involve themselves in transport but can usually arrange accommodation either in self-catering apartments or (the best) with local families. Expect to pay something like £225 each for half-board in a private house or £260 full board.

## Unusual Family Holiday No. 38: Ask The Experts

A good guide can really make a holiday. Someone who is master of a subject and can communicate it with enthusiasm. Places that had looked quite ordinary suddenly become fascinating and compelling once you know the stories behind them. Where kids are concerned the right, informal approach is vital. Classroom style lectures just won't go down well. You can do anything from a day to a fully inclusive two week tour and the range of possible subjects is endless. Pick something for which your kids already have an enthusiasm or, perhaps, a subject they're studying at school. You can tour battlefields, hunt for fossils, descend into volcanoes, meet native Americans, visit the homes of writers and artists...and just about anything you can think of. Incidentally, as a family you can also consider your very own private guide – if there are four of you or more you may find the prices quite competitive.

## FURTHER INFORMATION

For a travel directory that includes private guides in the UK see
**www.britainexpress.com**; for guide accompanied tours covering a wide
range of subjects from art and architecture to historical and battlefield sites to
cookery see **www.travelhistory.com**; for a directory of tours worldwide see
**www.infohub.com** Tel: 00 1 510 505 0931; for geology see
**www.bgs.ac.uk** Tel: 0115 936 3100 and **www.geologist.demon.co.uk**
Tel: 020 7434 9298.

### Some specialist operators

**www.andantetravels.co.uk** Tel: 01722 713 800

**www.pageandmoy.com** Tel: 0870 833 4012

**www.travelsphere.co.uk** Tel: 0870 240 2426

**www.atlastravelweb.com** Tel: 00 1 561 687 3301

**www.archaeology-safaris.co.uk** Tel: 07815 007 128

**www.astraltravels.co.uk** Tel: 0700 078 1016 (Harry Potter Tours)

**www.historyamerica.com** Tel: 00 1 972 769 1865

**www.decadevolcano.net**

**www.adventures-abroad.com** Tel: 0114 247 3400

**www.sydertravel.com** Tel: 01580 752 218

**www.rockwatch.org.uk** Tel: 020 7734 5398

**www.discoveringfossils.co.uk** Tel: 020 8772 8770

**www.fossilwalks.com** Tel: 01297 443 758

**www.leger.co.uk** Tel: 0845 458 55 99

**www.aigas.co.uk** Tel :01463 782 097

**www.smithsonianjourney.org** Tel: 00 1 877 338 8687

**www.nationalgeographicexpeditions.com** Tel: 00 1 888 966 8687

### Private tours

**www.xs4all.nl/~kalden** 00 31 206 698 119 (art, art history and
architecture)

**www.greek-museums.com** (Greek museums)

**www.newyorkpartyshuttle.com** Tel 00 1 212 277 8019 (New York)

## Some questions to ask

✓ Is this tour suitable for children?

✓ Are there likely to be other families on the tour?

✓ Does the guide speak good English?

✓ Will there be opportunities for relaxation or is it non-stop sightseeing?

## Why is this good for families?

The kids may not appreciate it at the time but they will later.

## Pros

- A stimulating supplement to school lessons.

## Cons

- Sightseeing holidays often don't leave much time for fun and games.

## Where to go

Fascinating subjects are everywhere with the right guide.

## When

Any time.

## Price guide

A five day coach tour of First World War battlefields with Leger costs from £220. For a private six hour tour of New York expect to pay around £250 for a family of four. The three day Hogwart's Express with Astral Travels costs around £350 (discounts for the under 12s). Eight days on Santorini with Decade Volcano costs around £550, not including flights. One week studying cave art in the Pyrenees with Andante costs around £1,400 per person full board, including flights.

# Unusual Family Holiday No. 39: Arty-Crafty Holidays

If you're an arty-crafty sort of family why not book an arty-crafty kind of holiday?

Photography is a great medium. Thanks to digital cameras, taking photographs is no longer the very expensive business it used to be (once, that is, you've bought the equipment). So it can be a marvellous hobby for all the family. But it's become a very technical medium, too.

What better way to learn all the techniques than on a photography holiday? Your teacher sets projects and off you all go, returning later in the day to download, analyse, edit and manipulate.

The best holidays, though, for families are probably those where a variety of media are on offer. How about doing something creative in the very garden where Claude Monet painted his famous water lilies? With ArtStudy-Giverny you can draw, paint and take photographs **www.artstudy.com** Tel: 00 33 2 32 21 96 83. And it doesn't stop there. You can study every kind of craft that there is from patchwork to furniture restoration.

## FURTHER INFORMATION

Just put the word 'holiday' together with your preferred medium and chosen destination into your search engine. You'll find links to art holiday specialists at **www.paintingholidaydirectory.com** and all sorts of useful information at **www.painting.about.com**. For links to photography courses take a look at **www.ephotozine.com/directories/listing.cfm?type=1**.

### Some specialist operators

#### Drawing and painting

**www.headwater.com** Tel: 01606 720 099 Various destinations.

**www.andalucian-adventures.co.uk** Tel: 01453 834 137 Spain.

**www.artinswfrance.com** Tel: 00 33 46 876 9882 France.

**www.paintinginitaly.com** Tel: 0800 458 9044 Italy.

**www.artworkshopitaly.com** Tel: 00 39 347 144 5342 Italy.

**www.rileyarts.com** Tel: 01803 722 352 Italy.

**www.paintgreece.com** Tel: 01424 712 968 Greece.

**www.artexchange-greece.com** Tel: 00 1 403 251 5297 Greece.

**www.artistacreative.com** Booking online California.

**www.farnecombeestate.co.uk** Tel: 0845 230 8590

**www.kunsthof-bahnitz.de** Tel 00 49 338 779 0714 Germany

#### Crafts

**www.boquio.com** Tel: 01209 831 694 UK. Ironwork and stained glass.

**www.lilacbarn.co.uk** Tel: 01823 690 134 UK. Patchwork and quilting.

Assington Mill Tel: 01787 229 955 UK. Furniture restoration.

**www.stonecarving.co.uk** Tel: 01547 528 792 Wales. Stone carving.

**www.florenceart.net** Tel: 00 39 055 714 033 Italy. Furniture decoration and gilding.

## Photography

**www.photoactive.co.uk** Tel: 01557 331 343

**www.peakphotocentre.com** Tel: 01298 687 211

**www.photoopportunity.co.uk** Tel: 020 7388 4500

**www.lightandland.co.uk** Tel: 01432 839 111

**www.lakelandphotohols.com** Tel: 01768 778 459

**www.wildshots.co.uk** Tel: 01540 651 352

**www.skyeinfocus.co.uk** 01471 822 264

**www.eileenoleary.com** Tel: 00 353 713 7429

**www.learninitaly.com** Tel: 041 535 1140

## Dance

**www.hfholidays.co.uk** Tel: 020 8905 9556

**www.bellydancingholidays.co.uk** Tel: 07956 286 166

**www.vivaflamencopromotions.com** Tel: 0870 011 3347

**www.partyweekender.com** Tel: 020 8593 1947

## Performing arts

**www.athenscentre.gr/theatre.htm** Tel: 00 30 210 701 2268

**www.singing-teachers.co.uk**

**www.angefou.co.uk** Tel: 020 7263 9339 (mime)

**www.jazzwise.com** Tel: 020 8769 7725

Singing Studio Tel: 020 7735 0532

## Cookery

**www.iceculinary/recreational/kids.shtml** Tel: 00 1 212 847 0770

**www.fontanadelpapa.it** Tel: 0039 7669 3455

## Why is this good for families?

If you're all creative there's no need to stop because you're on holiday.

## Some questions to ask

✓ Is this course suitable for children?

✓ What qualifications do your tutors have?

✓ What basic skills do we need?

✓ What is the tutor/student ratio?

✓ What mediums does the course cover?

✓ Do we need to bring materials/equipment?

✓ Will we be able to buy materials locally?

✓ How many others will be on the course?

✓ Is teaching done in a formal or informal way?

✓ How many hours of tuition will we receive each day?

✓ What other things are there to do in the area?

## Pros

● A new environment can be good for the creative juices.

## Cons

● Boring for anyone not overcome by creative passion.

## Where to go

Holiday courses are usually in areas of outstanding natural beauty.

## When

Courses are usually held in the summer.

## Price guide

Holiday courses in painting, crafts, photography and writing tend to cost from around £350 including lunch but no accommodation and from £500 a week half-board, whether in the UK or abroad, excluding travel. But they can go up to as much as £1,000. The two day furniture restoration course at Assington Mill, Suffolk costs just over £100, including lunch. The three day courses in forged iron or stained glass at Boquio Farm cost around £225 including lunch – or for £300 you can have undivided attention.

## Unusual Family Holiday No. 40: Teach Yourself Holidays

Nowadays self-improvement is all the thing and there are any numbers of books, CD-ROMs, online courses and all the rest. So if you're
the sort of family that likes to be independent you certainly don't need
to join a group led by a professional guide in order to learn. And with
the internet it couldn't be easier to book flights, hotels and whatever
else you need. Just make sure you do your homework before you set off.
In fact, you could give each member of the family a special project to
research and then lead.

### FURTHER INFORMATION

The £69 family membership of Historic Royal Palaces (**www.hrp.org.uk**)
gives you free entrance, special events and up to the minute news on five of
the UK's most important ancient buildings: Tower of London Tel: 0870
756 6060, Hampton Court Palace Tel: 0870 751 5175, Kensington
Palace Tel: 0870 751 5170, Banqueting House Tel: 0870 751 5178
and Kew Palace Tel: 0870 751 5179.

### Research your own itineraries

**www.information-britain.co.uk**

**www.nationaltrust.org.uk**

**www.enjoyengland.com**

**www.planetmyway.co.uk**

**www.historytravel.com**

**www.historichotels.org**

**www.famouslocations.com**

**http://whc.unesco.org**

**www.nationalgeographic.com**

**www.smithsonian.org**

**www.channel4.com/history/microsites/T/timeteam**

**www.world-mysteries.com**

**www.worldvacationrentals.net**

## Why is this good for families?

You can design an itinerary precisely tailored to your family's needs and interests.

## Pros

• See exactly what you want for as long as you want.

• Research before you go is part of the educational experience.

## Cons

• You may miss some things the professionals wouldn't.

• The holiday may not go as smoothly as the professional version.

## Where to go

Anywhere you want.

## When

Any time you want.

## Price guide

With a no frills airline, a self-drive car and a self-catering apartment a family of four could easily spend a week touring, for example, the prehistoric caves of the Pyrenees for under £1,000.

## Unusual Family Holiday No. 41: Voyages Of Discovery

We already talked about cruise ships in Chapter 4 so we're not going to say a lot more about them here. Other than to point out that cruising doesn't have to mean lying around. There's also a very different style with sailing time devoted to lectures rather than lounging. The 48 berth Grigoriy Mikheev will take you from Aberdeen to some of the remotest UK islands including Fair Isle, Mousa, Foula, North Rona, the Flannan Islands and St Kilda and you'll go ashore in inflatables – now that's not lying around **www.aigas.co.uk** Tel: 01463 782 443. Hebridean International, which cruises the Med and many other areas, has a list of guest speakers that reads like Who's Who? - Dr Charles Anderson, the marine biologist who worked on the BBC's Blue Planet, Richard Baker OBE who joined the BBC in 1950, Dr Peter Cattermole who lectures on volcanology and planetary geology, Sir Roy Strong, the curator and historian, and many others **www.hebridean.**

**co.uk** Tel: 01756 704 704. If your family has Viking blood then the Viking Voyage with Professor James Knirk of Oslo University could be for you, visiting Oslo, Trondheim, Svolvaer and Bergen **www.norwegiancoastalvoyage.com** Tel: 020 8846 2666. Even regular cruises now include a little intellectual stimulation. Princess Cruises has a 'Scholarship At Sea' programme (**www.crystalcruises-uk.com** Tel: 0800 008 6677) while Crystal has its 'Learning Institute' covering the performing arts, painting, art history, Asian woodblock printing, calligraphy, fashion design and writing (**www.princesscruises.co.uk** Tel: 0800 091 1629). And don't forget inland waterways. Go Barging, for example, will brush up your English history with a week on the Thames taking in Windsor Castle, Magna Carta Island and Hampton Court Palace **www.gobarging.com** Tel: 01784 482 439.

## FURTHER INFORMATION

For general advice see the online magazine **www.cruisemates.com** and the directory **www.thecruiseshop.co.uk** (Tel: 0800 074 6464). Other cruises with educational content are available from **www.deilmann.co.uk** Tel: 0845 310 4400, **www.swanhellenic.com** Tel: 0845 355 111, **www.fredolsencruises.co.uk** Tel: 01473 746 175, **www.noble-caledonia.co.uk** Tel: 020 7775 2000 and **www.rssc.com** Tel: 02380 682 297.

### Why is this good for families?
The benefits of cruising without anyone losing those 20 IQ points.

### Pros
- The sort of top rate lecturers you wouldn't normally have on holiday with you.

### Cons
- Not always enough shore time to study things in detail.

### Where to go
The Med is always good for historical/archaeological cruises.

### When
Normally summer.

## Price guide

Unfortunately, this kind of thing tends to be expensive. A week on the Grigoriy Mikheev, the Viking Voyage and barging on the Thames all cost around £2,000 a head.

## And finally

If you'd all like to learn how to drive nails up your noses, charm snakes and swallow swords then the Sideshow School at New York's Coney Island is for you. Full courses cost around £350 but one-off classes can also be arranged

**www.coneyislandusa.com/sideshow_school.shtml**
Tel: 00 1 718 372 5159.

# Chapter 10

# Fun With Fiestas

**Unusual family holidays in this chapter: carnivals, fireworks, festivals, processions, tugs of war, battle re-enactments and much more.**

If you really want to know what a country is like, go to one of its traditional fiestas. The kids will learn just as much as by visiting any museum. And it's a lot more fun, too. So, *que la fête commence*! Let's party!

## Unusual Family Holiday No. 42: It's Carnival Time

In Britain a carnival is a kind of procession and, given our weather, it's normally in the summer. But in much of the rest of the world carnival is a very specific thing, the period of merrymaking just before the rigours of the 40 days of Lent, and including Mardi Gras or 'Fat Tuesday' when all the fatty foods are eaten up prior to fasting. In Britain we call it Shrove Tuesday or Pancake Day. But with carnival usually falling in the latter part of February, what better excuse could there be for getting out of the country somewhere a little warmer – say, Venice, Nice, Cadiz or even Florida?

Here are some of the best:

**Venice**. There's a belief that Carnevale in Venice is only for the super rich and those with aristocratic connections but, in fact, there are plenty of free events. True, you could easily pay £350 each (plus obligatory costume hire) to get into one of the main balls. But, equally, there are masked parades in St Mark's Square, gondolier parades on the Grand Canal, huge fireworks displays and an impressive children's carnival in the Cannaregio district (which your own children can dress up for). Added value comes from the strange people walking around with masks and cloaks at all times of the day and night. For full details see **www.carnivalofvenice.com** or contact the Italian Tourist Board

**www.italiantouristboard.co.uk** Tel: 020 7408 1254. For costume hire you'll need to contact **www.veniceatelier.com**.

**Cologne**. Cologne's *Karneval* covers three days but, as they say in Cologne, they're *drei tollen Tage*. Crazy days! And they are. It's as if all inhibitions are suddenly set free and everybody – *everybody* – goes out on the streets costumed as their real selves, from clowns to reincarnations of Cleopatra (**www.colognecarnival.com** or **www.koeln.de**). It all begins on a Thursday (technically, the one prior to the seventh Sunday before Easter) with processions and costume balls. Then there's a two day lull before everything boils up to the *Rosenmontagzug* climax on the Monday, a procession featuring over a hundred bands, several hundred horses, thousands of people and probably a million sweets and chocolates thrown to the crowds. For an organised visit try **www.moswin.com.carnival.htm** Tel: 0870 062 5040

**Plaka, Athens**. The last two weekends of the Carnival period are particularly memorable. Walking the narrow streets you're liable to get bashed over the head with a squeaky plastic club (it doesn't usually hurt) of dubious historical origin and find confetti in your underwear. Children get to dress up and participate in fancy dress parades. On the final Monday (Clean Monday) most of Athens (it seems) takes to the green areas of the city to fly kites. Greek National Tourist Office **www.mintour.gr** Tel: 00 30 2103 310 392 or 020 7495 9300.

**Canary Islands**. The archipelago has strong links with the Caribbean and South America, giving its carnivals a distinctly 'Rio' flavour. The most important celebrations take place in Las Palmas and Santa Cruz de Tenerife, where the high spot is the election of the Queen of the Carnival. Some of the costumes are real feats of engineering wizardry. Information from **www.canaria-turismo.com** Tel: 00 34 922 239 811.

**Cadiz**. This city in Andalucia is renowned for its anarchic carnival, a reaction to the years of Franco's rule when carnival celebrations were banned. Hence there's always a political twist. Singing and dancing rules and everybody is encouraged to get into the spirit with fancy dress. See **www.andalucia.com** Tel: 00 34 956 211 313.

**Nice**. The narrow streets of Nice seethe with two million visitors for the two weeks of carnival. The event is famous for its floats and giants, its lights around the bay and a *grande finale* that includes fireworks and the burning of King Carnival **www.nicetourism.com** Tel: 00 33 49 392 8282.

**Limoux**. This town in the French Aude region is famous for its *goudils*, as the clowns in white satin costumes are known, who are liable to drag you into the street processions. Which is why it's a good idea for parents to partake of a little of the town's famous sparkling wine beforehand. On the final day the chosen King Carnival is burned with due ceremony **www.limoux.fr** Tel: 00 33 4 683 111 82.

**Ovar**. South American style carnival near Aveiro, Portugal, including a costumed children's parade. For dad, there are the samba schools with their fabulous but usually minimal outfits, and everybody loves the *carnavalescos* or jesters who interact with the crowd **www. visitportugal.com** Tel: 0845 355 1212 or **http://carnaval.ovar.net**.

**Hollywood**. Hollywood, Florida that is. For four days the streets are filled with entertainers and the beaches with parties **www.mardi grasfiesta.com** or **www.hollywoodfl.org** Tel: 00 1 954 921 3404.

**Olney, Buckinghamshire**. You may have never heard of it but Olney is in fact home to one of the UK's most important Shrove Tuesday celebrations – the Olney Pancake Race. In one form or another it goes back 500 years. At 11.55am exactly, women in pinnies, pancakes in frying pans, race the 415 yard course. At the finishing line the winner must successfully toss her pancake and get a kiss from the verger. Not to be missed **www.olneytowncouncil.co.uk** Tel: 01234 711 679.

## FURTHER INFORMATION

Some Carnival celebrations are more raucous than others and might be too boisterous for young children. For advice from those who have already been and done it try **www.tripadvisor.com**, **www.virtualtourist.com**, **www.tripconnect.com** or **www.holidaywatchdog.com**. Booked well enough in advance you can find some packages which, even if you are all out of fairy godmothers, means you can still all get to the ball.

### Some specialist operators

#### Italy

**www.citalia.com** Tel: 0870 909 7555

**www.classicitalia.com** Tel: 020 8663 3220

#### Germany

**www.dertravel.co.uk** Tel: 0870 142 0960

**www.german-travel-uk.com** Tel: 020 8429 2900

**www.taberhols.co.uk** Tel: 01274 594 656

**www.moswin.com.carnival.htm** Tel: 0870 062 5040

### Greece

**www.sunvilholidays.co.uk** Tel: 020 8568 4499

**www.citiesdirect.co.uk** Tel: 0870 442 1820

### Spain

**www.takemetocanaries.co.uk** Tel: 0970 220 3014

**www.tenerifetenerife.com** Tel: 020 8236 7099

### France

**www.insightvacations.com** Tel: 020 7468 4228

**www.europeanlife.co.uk** Tel: 0870 444 8800

### Portugal

**www.caravela.co.uk** Tel: 020 7630 5148

**www.portugalportugal.com** Tel: 020 8236 7092

### USA

**www.cosmosflorida.co.uk** Tel: 0870 443 5275

**www.travelcitydirect.com** Tel: 01293 498 200

### UK (Olney)

**www.hotels.uk.com/uk/buckinghamshire/hotels-olney.htm**

## Some questions to ask

✓ Is this carnival suitable for children?

✓ Is there a separate children's procession?

✓ Where's the best place to enjoy the procession?

✓ Are there any places it would be inadvisable to go with children?

✓ Will prices for food and accommodation be higher than usual?

## Why is this good for families?

Most carnivals are very family oriented

## Pros

- A good excuse to escape the British winter (or, at least, have a good laugh if you're staying for a British Shrove Tuesday).

## Cons

- Noisy, tiring and possibly expensive.

## Where to go

If none of the listed carnivals suit you, try **www.worldevents.com** and **www.carnaval.com**.

## When

Carnival usually falls between mid-February and late March.

## Price Guide

World famous events such as the Venice Carnival can be very expensive if you actually want to go to the balls (think hundreds of pounds), but there are free events, too. Generally, expect to pay summer prices even though it's winter.

# Unusual Family Holiday No. 43: The Frisson Of Fireworks

What child doesn't like fireworks? And, for some reason, adults seem to find them rather romantic. So they're the perfect family entertainment. And every year the displays get bigger, better and more elaborate.

Lets start with Guy Fawkes Night (5th November). You probably had fireworks in the garden when you were a kid but nowadays that's frowned upon. The best compensation you can possibly offer your children is at Lewes in East Sussex where the *bonfire boys* (as the local participants of the organising bonfire societies are known) are as subversive as Guy Fawkes was himself. From around 5pm until midnight torchlight processions weave from one bonfire to another where the most hated politicians and celebrities are burned (in effigy, of course) while the bonfire boys fight for firework supremacy **www.lewesbonfirecouncil.org**.

The other great fireworks displays in Britain are on the Isle of Wight for Cowes Week at the beginning of August and in Edinburgh at the beginning of September. The best place to enjoy Cowes, if you can possibly arrange it, is from the deck of a boat **www.skandiacowesweek.co.uk** Tel: 01983 813 813 (Tourist Office) or 01983 299 975 (Cowes Yacht Haven). For details of the Edinburgh International Festival of Fireworks see **www.edinburghfestivals.co.uk**. Of course, Edinburgh also has its Hogmanay (New Year) display (**www.edinburghshogmanay.org**) and we'll be taking a special look at that in Chapter 15.

The big firework night in France is Bastille Day, 14th July, when the best place to be is Paris. For the Spanish it's the eve of San Juan (the night of 23rd June), when every village and town celebrates midsummer/the birth of St John the Baptist with fireworks and bonfires. But the biggest displays in Spain are in Tarragona the first week in July and Valencia on 12th–19th March. For the Tarragona International Fireworks Competition six international fireworks companies are invited to compete above the Punta del Miracle on six successive nights **www.tarragona.piroart.com**. Valencia's Las Fallas (literally 'the fires' in Valencian) is the craziest of the lot. Neighbourhood organisations spend six months and tens of thousands of pounds building wood and cardboard statues called *ninots*, some of which are so heavy they have to be placed in position by cranes. They remain in place at 350 key locations around the city until the night of 19th March, known as *La Crema*, when they're stuffed with fireworks and set alight. Amazing but true **www.fallas.com** Tel: 00 34 963 524 000. If you miss it, there are some other smaller fallas, most notably in Alicante in June.

Even the USA on 4th July (Independence Day) has nothing to rival Las Fallas. But New York store Macy's has a good try. Its firework display attracts a live audience of two million with 12 million watching on TV (Tel: 00 1 212 695 4400). Another good city to be on 4th July is Tampa, Florida, where the display lasts 20 minutes and is choreographed to music. The city also has displays on all major holidays and Friday nights throughout the summer (Tel: 00 1 813 223 1111).

But the greatest *series* of fireworks displays in the *world* takes place on the Rhine and Mosel (**www.germany-tourism.co.uk** Tel: 00 49 179 250 6757). The season blasts off in May when a 26km stretch of the Rhine between Linz and Bonn is set aglow by 2000 'Bengal Fires'. Meanwhile, a fleet of 60 decorated and illuminated boats motors past and fireworks are set off at Linz, Remagen, Bad Honnef and, finally, Bonn itself.

Cologne (Koln) is a city that knows how to throw a party and the last Saturday in July is second only to the famous *Karneval*. Again there's a parade of boats followed by a 30 minute display from a Rhine barge anchored between the Deutz and Hohenzollern bridges.

In the middle of August it's the turn of Koblenz when some 80 barges take to the river and the fireworks are set off from the Stolsenfels castle and later in the night from the Ehrenbreitstein fortress at the mouth of the Mosel.

Next comes the 10 day wine festival at Winningen, always beginning on the last Friday in August and climaxing on the Sunday of the following week with *Die Mosel in Feuerzauber*, a firework display from a boat, creating an awesome cacophony in the Mosel Gorge.

Three more displays follow at Oberwesel, St Goar and St Goarshausen before Boppard finishes the season in emphatic style with *two* wine festivals and *two* displays – on the third weekend in September (Friday to Sunday) and the following weekend.

---

For major fireworks displays book your accommodation well in advance. The population of Valencia, for example, swells from half a million to three million for Las Fallas.

---

## FURTHER INFORMATION

For details of Guy Fawkes celebrations in Britain see **www.fireworks.co.uk** and **www.direct.gov.uk**. For a calendar of the world's major events take a look at **www.fireworksguide.com**.

### Some tour operators specialising in the Rhine/Mosel

**www.noble-caledonia.co.uk** Tel: 020 7752 0000

**www.peter-deilmann-river.cruises.co.uk** Tel: 020 7436 2931

**www.travelrenaissance.com** Tel: 01372 744 455

**www.travelscope.co.uk** Tel: 0870 380 3333

**www.taberhols.co.uk** Tel: 01274 594 656

**www.dertravel.co.uk** Tel: 0870 142 0960

### Some tour operators specialising in the USA

**www.virginholidays.co.uk** Tel: 0870 220 2788

**www.dreamusa.co.uk** Tel: 0800 856 0324

## Some questions to ask

✓ Where is the best place for children to watch from?

✓ How long does the display last?

✓ Where does everybody party afterwards?

## Why is this good for families?

All ages love fireworks.

## Pros

- A memorable climax to any holiday and usually free.

## Cons

- Celebrations such as Las Fallas can be very boisterous for small children.

- Can give you a crick in the neck.

## Price guide

An all inclusive package to watch fireworks on the Rhine costs from around £500.

# Unusual Family Holiday No. 44: VAT – Value Added Travel

The whole idea of value added travel is that you plan your holiday to coincide with a special event or happening. Here we list some of the best.

### Spring

Easter in Greece. Most towns and villages have candle parades. Feasts of lamb and eggs dyed red. Several areas, especially Crete, have huge bonfires on which effigies of Judas Iscariot are burnt **www.mintour.gr** Tel: 00 30 2 103 310 392 or 020 7495 9300.

23rd April – St George's Day. St George is not just the patron saint of England. At Lemnos and Crete in Greece, Catalonia in Spain, and Florence he is celebrated with candles, books, roses and sheep shearing **www.worldeventsguide.com**.

Late April. At Stockton, California, everything to do with asparagus is worshipped at the annual Asparagus Festival. For three days you can eat asparagus prepared by a succession of celebrity chefs, attend demonstrations of how to grow and cook it and listen to music, presumably played on asparagus **www.asparagusfest.com** or **www.visitcalifornia.com** Tel: 020 8237 7979.

Late April. In Los Angeles, the *Feria de los Niños* (Children's Festival) is a big, family oriented event with an Hispanic flavour, featuring tortilla making contests, dancing, puppetry and parades **www.laparks.org** Tel: 00 1 323 261 0113.

1st/2nd May. At Cagliari, Sardinia, the Feast of Saint Efisio includes one of the most ornate and longest parades in the world, led by the sacred statue of the saint, followed by ox carts, 'soldiers' on horseback, local dignitaries and hundreds of spectators. The two day walk ends at the Maddelena Beach, site of Efisio's martyrdom **www.sardi.it** or **www.italiantouristboard.co.uk** Tel: 020 7408 1254.

Mid-May. If your kids won't eat their fruit and vegetables then at the Family Artichoke Festival at Castroville, California, they'll at least learn how to make sculptures with them. Plus classic car shows, marching bands, parades and horse drawn floats. It's said that Marilyn Monroe launched her career at this festival **www.artichokefestival.org** Tel: 00 1 831 633 2465.

24th/25th May. Gypsies from all over Europe gather at Ste-Maries-de-la-Mer in the Camargue to venerate their patron saint, St Sarah. If anyone in the family is learning the guitar, it's a wonderful opportunity to experience impromptu and very authentic flamenco performances. The local 'cowboys' who herd the famous black bulls have their own pilgrimage at the same time **www.saintesmariesdelamer.com** Tel: 00 33 49 097 8255.

Late May/June. *Romerias* or pilgrimages take place all over Spain but that to the Virgen of Rocio in Andalucia is one of the biggest, attracting up to a million people, many on horseback or in horse drawn caravans. The noisy celebrations climax as the statue of the Virgin is brought out of the church **www.andalucia.com**.

Late May. If your family loves strawberries then they're going to have a great time at the annual Strawberry Festival at Arroyo Grande, California. Plenty of entertainment, too **www.arroyograndevillage.org** Tel: 00 1 805 473 2250.

Late May. Most children aren't very keen on mushrooms but the Morgan Hill Annual Mushroom Mardi Gras in California gets over that with plenty of other gourmet food, street entertainment and Munchkinland **www.mhmushroommardigras.com** Tel: 00 1 408 778 1786.

Late May. The Cheese Rolling at Gloucester has to rate as one of the world's most eccentric festivals. In each of four races (one is for women only), 20 competitors chase after an eight pound Double Gloucester cheese wheel as it gathers momentum down hill. The fastest wins the cheese. Lots of other entertainment, too **www.cheeserolling.co.uk**.

Late May. No kids could fail to enjoy the Festival of Fools at Muncaster Castle, Cumbria, said to be the home of the famous 17th century jester Thomas Skelton. Five days of general tomfoolery such as water fights, foolish football and stocks plus the staging of the International Jester Tournament. **www.muncaster.co.uk** Tel: 01229 717 614.

## Summer

Early June. The Cotswold Olimpick Games and Scuttlebrook Wake at Chipping Campden include such memorable events as the World Shin-Kicking Championships (audience participation voluntary) **www.olimpickgames.co.uk** Tel: 01384 274 041.

16th June. The Luminara in Pisa, Italy makes for a picturesque day out beside the River Arno, watching various regattas. At nightfall the riverbanks are lit up like fairyland **www.italiantouristboard.co.uk** Tel: 020 7408 1254.

June. Chester's Midsummer Watch Parade is a chance for your children to dress up in Tudor gear and take part in a historical pageant (you can, too) **www.chester.gov.uk** Tel: 01244 351 609.

June. A Hat Fair may not sound very exciting but this one is a chance for buskers from all over the world to play on the streets of Winchester and...pass the hat. Some of the acts are really very good. And if your holiday is proving a little expensive then just get the whole family busking **www.visitwinchester.co.uk** Tel: 01962 840 500.

Late June. If you have a son who plays rugby then he may be interested in the version played in Florence. Calcio Storico is played with a socking great stone between two beefy teams in fancy dress. Each team has 27 players and the game lasts 50 minutes. It's rough and occasionally bloody but the thousands of locals and visitors love it **www.calciostorico.it** or **www.enit.co.uk** Tel: 020 7408 1254

Late June. The Game of the Bridge involves two teams of 300-plus in fancy dress, each pulling a seven ton trolley across an historic bridge over the River Arno at Pisa, Italy **www.welcometuscany.it** Tourist Office Tel: 00 39 05 056 0464

Last weekend in June. The Miaouilis on Hydra celebrates a hero from the War of Independence, including the recreation of a naval battle in the town harbour, with some great fireworks. Not sure how the neighbours feel about the ritual burning of the Turkish flagship, though **www.mintour.gr** Tel: 00 30 210 331 0392 or 020 7495 9300.

Early July. We argued long and hard as to which was the craziest and most eccentric festival on the planet and eventually agreed that it had to be the Underwater Music Festival in Lower Keys, Florida. True, you have to be a diver (see Chapter 3) to fully appreciate this magnificent cultural event but the music is also transmitted via the local radio station. And there's plenty to do on dry land, too **www.fla-keys.com** or **www.lowerkeyschamber.com** Tel: 00 1 305 872 2411.

First week of August. The Sardine Festival at Kaloni on Lesbos – lots of fish, lots of wine and lots of dancing **www.mintour.gr** Tel: 00 30 210 331 0392 or 020 7495 9300.

Early August. Although the Inter-Celtic Festival is always held at Lorient, Brittany, a different Celtic nation 'hosts' the event every year. It attracts more than 600,000 visitors over 10 days. Highlights include the costume and flower parades **www.brittanytourism.com** Tel: 00 33 29 662 7201.

Early August. Every boy (and his dad) is going to love the Robin Hood Festival in Sherwood Forest, Nottinghamshire. A week long olde worlde fayre with jousting, archery, alchemy and all the usual stuffe, it's right goode.
But if you're rich, watch out **www.nottinghamshire.gov.uk**.

Early August. If your family isn't impressed by all that chucking of cabers then the Scottish Alternative Games at Castle Douglas could be for you. Highlights include throwing hats, snail racing and top spinning **www.scottish-alternative-games.com** or **www.dumgal.gov.uk** Tel: 01556 502 327.

15th August. Almost every town and village in Greece has its festival for the Day of Panagia (the Virgin Mary) **www.mintour.gr** Tel: 00 30 210 331 0392 or 020 7495 9300.

Mid-August. The Heart of the Glens Festival at Antrim, Ulster, including food tasting, sports, crafts and music **www.discovernorthernireland.com** or **www.nitb.org** Tel: 0282 1771 378.

Mid-August. Watch them get up, up and away in more than a hundred hot-air balloons at the International Balloon Fiesta, Bristol. Some of them are truly eccentric. On the ground there are stalls, stands and entertainment **www.visitbristol.co.uk** Tel: 0870 444 0654.

August Bank Holiday. Notting Hill Carnival. The biggest street festival in Europe with, on the Sunday, the best children's carnival **www.mynottinghill.com** and **www.portowebbo.co.uk** Tel: 020 7792 0624.

Last Wednesday of August. We don't recommend La Tomatina, Bunol near Valencia, for young children but teenagers just love this orgy of chucking overripe tomatoes at one another. So if you feel your kids are big enough to take a full grown Beef Tomato in the mush, and you don't mind it either, then this is something none of you will ever forget **www.communitatvalencia.com** Tel:00 34 963 649 506. For a specialist tour operator see **www.latomatina.com** Tel: 00 1 919 293 0105.

---

**Tip:** Wear swim goggles to protect your eyes.

---

## Autumn

First Sunday of September. This festival in Arezzo, Italy is one for the boys – a full scale jousting contest between armoured knights dressed in 13th century style **www.italiantouristboard.co.uk** Tel: 020 7408 1254.

First Sunday in September. Nowhere else in the world will you see anything like the Regata Storica, an incredible procession of outstanding historic boats along the Canal Grande in Venice, followed by a gondola race **www.italiantouristboard.co.uk** Tel: 020 7408 1254.

Early September. At the Wilderness Gathering Bushcraft Festival at West Knoyle, Wiltshire your family can learn everything necessary for a cheap holiday living off the land. Demonstrations and workshops in various unusual skills. **www.wildernessgathering.co.uk** Tel: 01580 882 194.

Early September. The Goodwood Festival in West Sussex will take you all back to the early days of motor racing – fancy dress, historic car rallies, famous motor racing faces, good old fish and chips, plus a fairground **www.goodwood.co.uk** Tel: 01243 755 055.

Early September. A huge number of weird and wonderful flying contraptions are demonstrated throughout the weekend at the Bristol Kite Festival. Just make sure you don't get carried away

**www.kite-festival.org** and **www.visitbristol.co.uk** Tel: 0870 444 0654.

Early September. The International Bognor Birdman Weekend provides a substantial £25,000 prize for the longest flight in an inevitably weird flying machine. Safest as a spectator sport **www.birdman.org.uk**.

Mid-September. It's glorious and there's nothing quite like it for cooling the blood, as everyone can discover for themselves at the National Mud Festival of Wales at Llanelli. So get down there for (amongst other things) the slippery tug of war, welly wanging, mud carving, face packs and pottery classes **www.wwt.org.uk/visit/llanelli** Tel: 01554 741 087.

Mid-September. The infamous gurning (face pulling to you and me) and greasy pole climbing are just two of the intellectually-stimulating events at the Egremont Crab Fair, Cumbria **www. egremontcrabfair.org.uk** Tel:01946 824052.

Mid-September. Every two years, the Living Chess Game at Marostica, Italy enacts a 15th century love story, complete with fully costumed actors, musicians and story tellers **www.marosticascacchi.it** Tel: 00 39 042 472 127.

Mid-September. The Black Pudding Throwing World Championship is held at the Royal Oak Public House, Ramsbottom, near Bury, attracting 800 contenders from around the world. In front of an audience of thousands, they compete to see who can knock the most Yorkshire Puddings out of a 20ft high pile with three underarm throws of a standard six ounce black pudding **www.bury.gov.uk** Tel: 0161 253 5000 or 01706 822 786 (Royal Oak).

Mid-September. The Annual Food Festival at Abergavenny, Wales, has been rated the UK's number one food event – visiting celebrities, idiosyncratic food preparation, a special children's area, plenty to eat and not a crisp in sight **www.abergavennyfoodfestival.com** Tel: 01873 850 805.

Late September. Sainte Hilaire du Touvet near Grenoble, France. Daft flying machines and even dafter pilots take to the air (or don't) at the Icarus Cup, which is awarded to the lengthiest flight. The four day event also has conventional air displays, films and a flea market for finding rare spare parts **www.sainthilairedutouvet.com** or **www. coupe-icare.org** Tel: 00 33 47 608 3399

All September. Spread out over the month, the Brighton Food Festival includes special children's events **www.brightonfoodfestival.co.uk** Tel: 01273 207 155.

Early October. Three days of avocado inspired eating, drinking and making merry at the Annual Avocado Festival, Carpinteria, California **www.avofest.com**.

Early October. Is Mum's porridge the best in the world? Find out at The Golden Spurtle World Porridge making Championships at Carrbridge, Scotland. Cash prizes for the chef making the finest traditional porridge (oatmeal, water and salt only) or a speciality porridge (with anything added). Other events include fun runs, farmer's markets, all things edible in oatmeal, and music **www.highlandfeast.co.uk** Tel: 01463 222 915.

Mid-October-early November. National Gastronomic Festival, Santarem, Portugal (about 50 miles north-east of Lisbon). A sumptuous feast of traditional Portuguese food and wine tasting, washed down with music and dancing **www.rtmbalejo.org** Tel: 00 351 243 330 330.

Mid-November. Of all the food festivals the International Chocolate Festival at Obidos near Lisbon, Portugal, is the one most likely to appeal to children. Sculpture competitions, cookery master classes and loads of tastings **www.festivalchocolate.cm-obidos.pt** Tel: 00 351 262 955 561.

## Winter

23rd December. The festival of Kladaries at Kozani, Greece, remembers the story of the shepherds who lit bonfires to announce the birth of Jesus. Now villagers light the fires and have a party and the best bonfire is awarded a prize **www.mintour.gr** Tel: 00 30 210 331 0392 or 020 7495 9300.

31st December. Local fishermen at Chios, Greece, parade with model ships singing songs of the sea. The models are later judged in the town square and awards given **www.mintour.gr** Tel: 00 30 210 331 0392 or 020 7495 9300.

8th January. In Thrace (Greece) women get their revenge on men during the one day of *Gynaecocratia*. Mums, you'll be able to go into all those bars that for 364 days of the year are the exclusive preserve of men, leaving your other half back at the hotel washing clothes. Your Greek sisters will be doing the same. At nightfall the two sexes come together in an amicable celebration – after which, it's life as normal **www.mintour.gr** Tel: 00 30 210 331 0392 or 020 7495 9300.

Mid-January. Enjoy California's favourite dishes at the Winter Fancy Food Show, San Francisco **www.specialityfood.com**.

Mid-February. You probably didn't know that they grow dates in California, and at the National Date Festival at Indio they even have camels and ostriches, too **www.datefest.com** Tel: 1 800811FAIR (within USA only).

17th March. As anybody faintly Irish knows, it's the birthday of the chief paddy, St Pat and what better place to be on St Patrick's Day than Dublin? As you may imagine, Guinness isn't far from many revellers' thoughts but there are plenty of things for children, too, including street parades, music and dancing **www.stpatricksfestival.ie** Tel: 00 353 1676 3205.

25th March. Greek National Anniversary Day is one long series of parties and street parades **www.mintour.gr** Tel: 00 30 210 331 0392 or 020 7495 9300.

## FURTHER INFORMATION

The rule is to book early and, if you really want to get into the swing of things, to have a hotel or self-catering apartment in the middle of the action, preferably one with a view over the processions or activities. More information and ideas can be found at

**www.greektravel.com, http://goitaly.about.com, http://gofrance.about.com, www.localfestivals.com, www.information-britain.co.uk, www.efestivals.co.uk** and **www.worldeventsguide.com**.

## Some questions to ask

✓ Is this an event that's suitable for children?

✓ Are there special children's areas or activities?

✓ Do dates change year by year?

✓ Where is our accommodation in relation to the celebrations?

✓ Will I be able to travel in and out of the area by car?

✓ Do we have to pay for entrance to events?

✓ Are there other family-friendly things to do in the area?

## Why is this good for families?

Most events have a wide family appeal so you should all be happy.

## Pros

- A festival is the pulse of a nation and a memorable highlight to any holiday.

## Cons

- Crowds may make it difficult to see the other sights.

## Price Guide

For the really big festivals food and accommodation prices may be considerably higher than normal.

## And finally

Re-enactments of battles between Christians and Moors take place in some 150 towns and villages around Spain at different times of the year. Some of them are extremely impressive, involving hundreds of people in authentic costume. One of the best is at Alcoy in April, where a papier maché castle is erected in the square **www.cb2000.net** Tel: 00 34 965 634 606. Cartagena has a slightly different version when the locals fight the 'Romans' over 10 days in September or October **www.carthaginesesyromanos.com** Tel: 00 34 968 506 483. Other good locations include Valencia, Elche, Granada, Toledo, Cádiz and Jaén.

# Chapter 11

# Unusual Theme Parks

**Unusual family holidays in this chapter: Europa-Park, Gardaland, Tivoli, Puy du Fou, Futuroscope and much more.**

There's nothing very unusual about going to a theme park. Just about everybody who goes to America visits one. It's what you do in America. But there's no need to go as far as the USA. There are some fantastic theme parks in Europe, too, which are not very well known. In fact, Forbes Magazine recently named *six* European theme parks as among the top 10 most fun in the world. Only three were in the USA and the other was in South Korea.

## Unusual Family Holiday No. 45: Europa-Park.

What's the most popular theme park in Europe? Maybe Disneyland Paris? No prizes for guessing that. But what's the second most popular? We'll give you a clue. It's in Germany, between Freiburg and Strasbourg. Give up? It's Europa-Park.

If you've never heard of it that's not altogether surprising because it's not in a hugely popular holiday area for British families. On the other hand, there's plenty else for outdoor minded families with a car to do in the area. There's the Black Forest and the Vosges for a start. So Europa-Park could be a dedicated short break or part of a touring holiday in the region.

What made Forbes put Europa-Park in its top 10? Opened back in 1975 it's built up an impressive collection of nine roller coasters of which the latest, *Pegasus*, opened in 2006. Highlights include *Euro Mir,* which recreates the sensation of being on a Russian Space Mission (while, next door, there's a walk through of the Mir training module); and *Silver Star*, Europe's highest roller coaster (for the moment) and the second fastest.

Every day there are numerous shows, including an ice show, an acrobatics show, a gladiator show and a 4D cinema.

Accommodation ranges from the tipi village, which works out at around £10 a head per night, up to well over £100 each. The Colosseo, the largest hotel, is a sort of recreation of the Coliseum in Rome.

### FURTHER INFORMATION

Tour operators offering Europa-Park include Leger Holidays **www.leger.co.uk** Tel: 0845 402 0360 and DER Travel Service www.dertravel.co.uk Tel: 0870 142 0960.

**www.europapark.de** Tel: 00 49 0 18 05 77 66 88

## Unusual Family Holiday No. 46: Gardaland

Gardaland is Italy's leading theme park. Situated on the shores of Lake Garda, it can be part of a 'lakes and mountains' holiday and even combined with the Verona Opera Festival (Chapter 8) and a visit to Venice. On a site of 46 hectares it offers 38 rides and attractions and gets more than three million visitors a year.

Highlights include *The Corsairs*, a boat ride past sea serpents and fighting pirate ships; *Escape from Atlantis*, with one of the highest artificial waterfalls in Europe; *Blue Tornado*, simulating a flight in a fighter plane; and *Space Vertigo*, a 40m freefall.

The onsite hotel offers 11 different shows every day and has a choice of five restaurants.

### FURTHER INFORMATION

**www.gardaland.it/en** Tel: 00 39 045 644 9777

## Unusual Family Holiday No. 47: Tivoli Gardens

The Tivoli Gardens in Copenhagen date back to 1843 but their quaint image has long been superseded by high tech rides. Apparently, the founder sold the idea to King Christian VIII on the philosophy that 'when the people are amusing themselves they do not think about politics.' Politics will certainly be the last thing on the minds of you all as you ride the *Demon* roller coaster which features an Immelmann loop and a Zero-G roll. But the traditional touches remain, like the

*Rutchebanen*, one of the world's oldest wooden rollercoasters still in operation – it dates from 1914. Tivoli also features the world's tallest carousel (the *Himmelskibet*) which swings you around at a stomach churning 80m from *terra firma*.

**www.tivoli.dk/** Tel: 00 45 3315 1001

## Unusual Family Holiday No. 48: Puy du Fou

Puy Du Fou is not so much about rides as history – the most exciting bits – brought to life. The scale of it has to be seen to be believed and if your kids say history is boring they'll definitely change their minds after this. There's a 6,000 seat Roman amphitheatre, of which the Romans themselves would have been proud, with gladiatorial combat and chariot racing. There's jousting. Musketeers swashing their buckles. Castles being bombarded and catching fire. And at night (which is extra) there's what's claimed to be the world's biggest night time show involving more than 1,000 actors, 5,000 costumes and a 'stage' which covers 23 hectares. In 2007 a three star hotel opened on the site, modelled on a 'gallo-roman villa' (although, hopefully, not the plumbing). Puy du Fou is in the Vendée region of France, about 45 miles southeast of Nantes, which means that, with a car, there are plenty of other things to do, including a visit to La Rochelle and the coast as well as Futuroscope near Poitiers (see next entry).

**www.puydufou.com/uk/** Tel: 00 33 2 51 64 11 11 (Hotel Tel: 00 33 2 51 64 11 11)

## Unusual Family Holiday No. 49: Futuroscope

Like Puy Du Fou, Futuroscope isn't about rides so much as experiences. But here they're simulated. *Destination Cosmos* sits you in front of a dome screen and for 25 minutes takes you on a journey to the stars. It's fascinating, mind boggling stuff and every kid will want to be an astronaut afterwards. *Peril On Akryls* is one of those simulators that convinces you you're flying and tilting and banking when, in fact, you've never moved from the spot. But if you do want to move, try *Dances With Robots* which sits you on huge, articulated, computer controlled arms as they, indeed, dance. Other attractions include an IMAX cinema showing *Young Black Stallion* and a whole galaxy of big screen interactive games for individuals and teams.

**www.futuroscope.com** Tel: 00 33 5 49 49 11 12

## Unusual Family Holiday No. 50: Warner Bros. Movie World

Spain's Port Aventura near Tarragona is one of Forbes Magazine's top 10 theme parks in the world but we decided it's too well known to rate an 'unusual' tag. We've opted instead for the Warner Bros. Movie World theme park near Madrid which you enter via Hollywood Boulevard. One of the top rides is the 58m high *Stuntfall* which the cognoscenti say is the same as Déjà Vu at Six Flags. Knowing that could save you a long trip across the Atlantic. Batman will invert you five times and, if that's not enough, Superman will do it seven times, at speeds approaching 60 miles an hour. As you'd expect of a movie theme park there are lots of shows, including the inevitable wild west shoot out, Batman, jet skis leaping all over the place, Looney Tunes characters and a demonstration of the secrets of film make-up. The service is very American, that's to say, excellent. When you've finished at the park there are still all the sights of Madrid, plus Toledo (the greatest medieval city of Spain) and the royal palaces and gardens at Aranjuez (which so inspired the composer Rodrigo). Hotels in the area include the Barcelo Aranjuez.

**www.warnerbrospark.com** Tel: 00 34 918 211 300

## Unusual Family Holiday No. 51: Phantasialand

Phantasialand at Bruhl near Cologne is Germany's second most important theme park and many people think it's the best. By popular consent, *Black Mamba*, an inverted coaster with an African theme, is the top ride. Others include *Galaxy*, one of the largest simulators in the world; *Colorado Adventure*, a runaway mine train through the mountains; *River Quest*, a rafting adventure, and *Mystery Castle*, a unique free fall inside a castle tower. Many of the rides are indoors, which means that bad weather needn't spoil the holiday. Phantasialand also has a good reputation for its various shows which include some incredible stunts, ice-skating and a 4D cinema.

Eating is as varied as the rides, including German, Mexican, Chinese and Italian cuisine. And at night you can lie down in a Chinese themed room in the four star Hotel Phantasia – it's so authentic that even the roof tiles were imported from China. Naturally there are Chinese gardens as well as a pool, a spa and two restaurants.

Things to do afterwards include visit Cologne and tour down the Rhine, with its famous castles.

**www.phantasialand.de**

## FURTHER INFORMATION

Theme Park Insider gives details of accidents at theme parks as well as readers' opinions of the rides and attractions
**www.themeparkinsider.com**. For travel to theme parks see
**www.themeparktravel.co.uk** Tel: 0845 003 2212.

### Some other unusual theme parks

**www.secretbunker.co.uk** Tel: 01333 310 301 UK.

**www.gulliversfun.co.uk** Tel: 01925 230 088 UK.

**www.vulcania.com** Tel: 00 33 8 20 82 78 28 France.

**www.andalucia.com** Tel: 00 34 950 365 236/00 34 950 165 456 for Mini Hollywood/Texas Hollywood, Spain.

**www.fortfun.de** Tel: 00 49 290 5810 Germany.

**www.filmpark.de** Tel: 00 49 3317 212 755 Germany.

**www.silverlakecity.de** Tel: 00 49 3987 20840 Germany.

**www.medievaltimes.com** Tel: 00 1 800 229 8300 Florida.

**www.hernandoheritagemuseum.com** Tel: 00 1 352 799 0129 Florida.

**www.sixflags.com** Tel: 00 1 805 255 411 California.

**www.knotts.com** Tel: 00 1 714 220 5200 California.

**www.pgathrills.com** Tel: 00 1 408 986 1776 Ext.8858 California.

**www.bonfantegardens.com** Tel: 00 1 408 8407 100 California.

**www.astroland.com** Tel: 00 1 718 372 025 New York.

### Some questions to ask

✓ Are there child care facilities?

✓ Is there a babysitting service?

✓ Is there a medical centre on site?

✓ How old/tall do you have to be for the rides?

✓ Have there been any serious accidents?

✓ What happens if it rains?

### Why is this good for families?

As far as kids are concerned, a theme park can more than make up for all the boring things adults insist on doing on holiday.

### Pros

- Designed by experts to keep children (and adults) happy.

### Cons

- Lots of queuing at busy times.
- Expensive.

### Where to go

The USA and especially California is the home of the theme park but Europe's best parks have now caught up.

### When

Mostly summer but many theme parks now reopen for the Christmas season.

### Price guide

The entrance to the big American theme parks costs around £30 at the gate but there are usually special deals (such as two days for the price of one). *Quite often prices are significantly cheaper if booked online.* Warner Bros in Madrid costs around £25 for adults and £18 for children five to 11; Futuroscope is around £22 for adults and £17 for children; Puy du Fou costs around £18 a day for adults and £11 for children three to 11(£30 and £17 including the night time show).

---

## And finally

The Forbidden Corner near Leyburn in North Yorkshire is not so much a big theme park as an Indiana Jones style underground labyrinth entered through a giant mouth. Families have to solve clues, complete challenges and negotiate obstacles such as the stepping stones, the glass pyramid and statues squirting water if they're ever to emerge. It's been voted the best kids' attraction in Yorkshire and, given the small number of people it can cope with, booking is essential. Adults £7.50; children 3 – 15 £5.50; under threes free **www.yorkshirenet.co.uk/theforbiddencorner** Tel: 01969 640 638.

# Chapter 12

# Single Parent Holidays

**Unusual single parent holidays in this chapter: lone parent clubs and support groups, making friends abroad, home swaps and much more.**

Holidays aren't easy for single parents. You just can't have a minute to yourself. You can't even risk snoozing on the beach because there's no one else to keep an eye on the children. And it's easy to feel lonely. But, then, not to worry because you probably can't afford a holiday in the first place.

Well, in fact, you probably can if you go about it the right way. Here are some suggestions:

It may not sound like the ideal holiday but sometimes you have no choice but to rope in family and friends – a sister, perhaps, or your parents. Or, better still, another single parent you know through school. You can share responsibility as well as the cost of things like self-catering accommodation and car hire.

Join Gingerbread, the largest UK charity for lone parents and their children. Gingerbread not only organises holidays but with some 12,000 members it has over 200 local self-help groups **www. gingerbread.org.uk** Tel: 0800 018 4318.

Join HELP (Holiday Endeavour for Lone Parents). HELP is a charity that specialises in low cost and subsidised holidays in the UK and Spain with major companies. Membership costs £3. Tel: 01302 728 791.

Join **www.spiceuk.com** which organises all kinds of activities for all kinds of people, lone parents included.

Consult **www.lone-parents.org.uk** for all kinds of helpful information, holidays included.

Go to a hotel, camp or resort where there are children's clubs (see Chapter 4). Companies like Sunsail, Neilson and Esprit Holidays are good. But that's going to leave you on your own much of the day so be sure you can cope with that.

Travel with a specialist lone parent tour operator. Normally there's plenty of support and, of course, you'll be with lots of other single parents and their children. Some ideas are given below.

## Unusual (Single Parent) Family Holiday No. 52: Specialist Operators

You know what it's like. You're in a crowd but you feel all alone. That's the reality for many single parents taking their broods along on what claim to be holidays suitable for all families but which in reality only cater for the standard Mum, Dad and juniors. It's not just the nuisance of having to pay a single room supplement, it's also feeling isolated and hands on 24/7, despite being surrounded by people. Fortunately several holiday operators spotted this problem (often through personal experience) and now there are special lone parent family holidays both in the UK and abroad.

This is still a fairly new field and there isn't yet much depth to it. Don't expect single parent family diving holidays or riding holidays, for example, but if you're looking for regular beach holidays in destinations like Spain, Portugal and Greece this could be the solution. You'll be in a group composed exclusively of other single parents and you'll have the choice of doing things all together, or with just one other family you've made friends with, or as a family on your own. Usually you'll be able to make arrangements with the other single parents so you can each have times to yourselves and there's normally a courier to ease things along.

### FURTHER INFORMATION

Put 'single parent', 'lone-parent' or 'one-parent' into your search engine together with the word 'holiday' and your chosen destination if you have one. The holiday directory Travel-Quest (**www.travel-quest.co.uk** ) has a special section on 'single-parent families'. If you're interested in the USA see **www.singleparenttravel.net**. For cruising see Chapter 4.

### Some specialist operators

**www.smallfamilies.co.uk** Tel: 01767 650 312

**www.mangokids.co.uk** Tel: 01902 373 410

**www.singleparentsonholiday.co.uk** Tel: 0871 550 4053

**http://members.aol.com/opfholiday** Tel: 01361 810 710

**www.vacationstogo.com** Tel: 0800 279 8084

**www.responsibletravel.com** Tel: 01273 600 030

## Some questions to ask

✓ How big are the groups?

✓ Are there organised events?

✓ Are we expected to attend the organised events?

✓ Will there be opportunities for single parents to socialise without the kids?

✓ Will I be able to have some time to myself?

## Why is this good for a single parent family?

Because everybody keeps an eye on everybody else's kids so each parent can enjoy a little free time.

## Pros

- You'll be with other people who understand your situation.
- You won't be shut out by self-sufficient couples.
- You'll be guaranteed the chance to socialise with other single adults of both sexes.

## Cons

- There's not a huge range of choice at the moment.

## Where to go

The range of destinations focuses mainly on the UK, Spain, Portugal, Greece and the USA.

## When

School holidays of course (not forgetting half-term).

## Price Guide

A five day UK all inclusive holiday costs from around £200 per child and £300 for a parent with Mango; seven nights on Crete in a four star hotel half-board cost from £370 for a child under 12 and from £470 for a parent.

## Unusual (Single Parent) Family Holiday No. 53: Friends Abroad

When you're a single parent it's really nice to be able to stay with a friend, especially another single parent. And even better if that friend lives in, say, Florida or Spain. Great for those that have them. But how do you make friends abroad?

Usually it's something that if it happens at all it happens by accident. But there are also specific things you can do to make friends. Some internet sites are dedicated to pen pals whose aim, quite openly, is to travel (for example, **www.meeturplanet.com** and **www.hospitalityclub. org**). Members post profiles of themselves on the site and establish initial contact by e-mail. Of course, they tend to be single people without children but that doesn't mean they wouldn't be willing to host you and your children. It's worth a try. In return they'll be wanting to come and stay with you, of course. Being a member imposes no obligation but if you want to be a traveller it's only fair that you should also be willing to be a host.

Other pen pal sites don't necessarily have cheap travel as their aim but it's only natural that, if all goes well, you'll want to visit one another. Alternatively, just make friends through internet chatrooms for any subject that interests you.

Of course, this isn't the kind of thing to try a couple of weeks before your holiday. You need to start making contact perhaps a year in advance so you can really get a feel for one another.

### FURTHER INFORMATION

### Some specialist sites

**www.friendsabroad.com** – essentially for pen pals to practise language skills.

**www.penpalworld.com** – dating as well as friendship.

**www.pen-pals.net/** - dating as well as friendship.

**www.europa-pages.com/penpal_form.html** – a serious site, not for dating.

**www.unitedplanet.org** – all kinds of open discussions with people who share your interests.

## Some questions to ask

✓ Every kind of question to try to find out what you have in common and establish a rapport.

✓ Would you (and your children) like to come and stay with us?

✓ We're planning to visit Spain/Italy/Florida etc and we'd like to meet up with you.

## Why is this good for a single parent family?

When you hook up with another family you're no longer alone.

## Pros

- You save money.
- You get an insider's view of the destination
- You make friends.

## Cons

- You might not get on when you actually meet.

## Where to go

Wherever you want.

## When

Whenever you want.

## Price guide

You won't be paying anything for accommodation but you'll still have to pay for fares and, of course, you'll have to make a contribution to food etc.

## WARNING

Some people on pen pal internet sites and chatrooms are only interested in sex – cyber or real. Others are seeking marriage as a way of escaping a harsh economic and/or political situation. Make it very clear that you're only interested in contacting people who share your interests and outlook with a view to friendship between two families.

## Unusual Family Holiday No. 54: Home Swapping

There is an obvious way of saving money on accommodation. It's called home swapping. And when you think about it, it makes a lot of sense. All you have to do is find a family – single parent or otherwise – that would like to take a holiday in your town while you spend a holiday in their town. No hotel bills. And no reason your food bill should be much different to the usual. So that only leaves transport to pay for.

But how are you ever going to find such a family? Well, thanks to the internet it's a whole lot easier than you might have imagined. All you have to do is sign up with a specialist agency. You then have access to their online register of destinations and properties. At the same time, other people will be able to see what you have to offer.

House swapping isn't something you can rush at. You'll need to register months ahead of your holiday date. They'll be wanting to feel you out and you'll be wanting to feel them out. It takes time.

Different people take different attitudes to their homes. If everything in your home is precious to you then maybe you shouldn't take the risk. If, on the other hand, you take the view that experiences are more important than possessions (which can usually be replaced, anyway) then home swapping could be your thing. Your children, on the other hand, might not be very keen on the idea of someone else sleeping in their bedroom. Children can be even more possessive and territorial than adults. Explain the idea to them, involve them and make sure they're comfortable about everything before you go ahead.

However relaxed you are you'll probably have some possessions you regard as highly personal and that you'll want to lock away. Certain clothes, perhaps, private papers, photographs, home videos – whatever. If your house is large enough you may be able to put these into a room which will then be locked. In any event, you'll have to clear out a certain amount of storage space for your guests.

Once you've decided to do it try to be relaxed. A few things are bound to get broken. Just accept the idea. Budget for it. And don't get too nit-picking over quid pro quo. A perfect match is impossible. Almost inevitably one party will be getting a home slightly less luxurious than their own. If it's you just accept it philosophically.

## FURTHER INFORMATION

Put 'house swap' into your search engine. With most specialist agencies you can see at least a sample of the properties registered before signing up. It helps to be flexible and interested in a range of destinations rather than just one. If you decide to go ahead, get as much advice as you can from the house swap agency and, if possible, from anybody who's done a house swap.

### Some specialist agencies

**www.homelink.org**

**www.homebase-hols.com**

**www.homeexchange.com**

**www.another-home.com**

**www.swapeo.com**

**www.swaphouse.org/eng**

### Some questions to ask

✓ Every kind of question to try to find out what you have in common and establish a rapport.

✓ What happens if there's a problem with either home?

✓ What about gardening and normal maintenance?

✓ What will we do about post that arrives during the holiday period?

✓ Shall we look after one another's pets?

✓ Shall we 'swap' cars, too? If yes, what about motor insurance?

✓ What about insurance for damage?

✓ What shall we do about running costs — electricity, gas and so on?

✓ What about telephones?

### Why is this good for a single parent family?

Saving money is the number one consideration but staying in a house or apartment can also be more relaxing than a hotel.

### Pros

• A cheap holiday.

- Environmentally friendly — no empty houses.
- Hopefully your co-swappers will be looking after your house, garden and pets while you're away.

### Cons

- Your home might get damaged (annoying).
- Their home might get damaged (embarrassing).

### Where to go

Wherever you want.

### When

Whenever you want.

### Price guide

You won't be paying anything for accommodation but you'll still have to pay for fares, food etc. Membership of a home swap organisation is quite cheap — from around £30 a year up to around £75.

## And finally

If you want to get a taste of what the specialist lone parent tour operators are like why not try a short break? Small Families, for example, runs a party weekend in the UK for past and potential clients, including a treasure hunt for the kids, a child friendly disco and a party night **www.smallfamilies.co.uk** Tel: 01767 650 312.

# Chapter 13

# Holidays For Children With Disabilities

**Unusual family holidays in this chapter: snorkelling, diving, skiing, swimming with dolphins, riding, sailing and much more.**

If you're the parent of a child with disabilities then you'll know very well that your child is capable of far more than other people imagine. But he or she may also be capable of far more than you imagine. So for this chapter we made a particular point of investigating some of the most unlikely seeming holidays. Here there are ideas that many able-bodied adults would think twice about. But we've seen children with disabilities doing them and having a marvellous time. Some are mostly for pleasure but others combine fun with a therapeutic element as well.

To begin with, here are some useful contacts:

## General:

**www.direct.gov.uk/disability**

**www.3hfund.org.uk** Tel: 01892 547 474 – grants for travel.

**www.radar.org.uk** Tel: 020 7200 3220 – general information about disabilites.

**www.bcodp.org.uk** Tel: 01332 295 551 – UK Disabled People's Council.

**www.adapt-europe.org**

**www.abilityplus.org** (USA) Tel: 00 1 603 236 4758

## Advice on suitable activities:

**www.disabilitysport.org.uk**

**www.efds.net** Tel: 0161 247 5294 – English Federation of Disability Sport.

**www.fdsp.co.uk** Tel: 01924 279 305 – Federation of Disability Sports.

**www.handiconcept.com** (Switzerland) Tel 00 41 79 240 7082

**www.handisport.org** Tel: 00 33 14 031 4500 – directory.

**www.spokenmotion.com** – useful links throughout the world.

## Holidays and holiday advice:

**www.disabledholidaydirectory.co.uk** – online directory of companies specialising in holidays for the disabled.

**www.accessatlast.com** Tel: 0845 890 2120 – information on accommodation and transport for the disabled.

**www.ability.org.uk** – directory.

**www.vitalise.org.uk** Tel: 0845 330 0149 – short breaks for disabled people and their carers.

**www.jet-smart.com** Tel: 01252 526 200 – private jet travel for the disabled.

**www.access-able.com** – USA holiday site for the disabled.

**www.caravanclub.co.uk** Tel: 01342 326 944 – information about disabled access to sites both at home and abroad.

**www.campingandcaravanningclub.co.uk** Tel: 0845 130 7632

**www.caravan-sitefinder.co.uk/features/disabled** Tel: 0845 644 4185

**www.optionholidays.co.uk** Tel: 01285 740 491

**www.disabilitytravel.com** Tel: 00 1 610 521 0339

**www.wheelgotravelling.info** – private and inspiring site about travelling with a wheelchair.

**www.break-charity.org** Tel: 01263 822 161

**www.rbf-products.co.uk** A bean bag insert that fits in an aircraft seat (with holes for seatbelt) which can be moulded round the body.

**www.crellings.com** A chest harness which loops over the back of the seat.

## Unusual Family Holiday (Including Children With Disabilities) No. 55: Diving And Snorkelling

Given that diving is a potentially hazardous sport it might seem surprising that we're suggesting it for children at all, let alone those with disabilities. But in fact the weightless undersea world is precisely the environment that can give back to many disabled children the mobility they've lost. We've seen children diving with just one leg, for example, and paraplegic youngsters performing the same manoeuvres – the rolls and loops and so on – as the able-bodied. Underwater, certain disabilities just don't matter as much as they do on land.

It's normal for divers to use fins for propulsion, for example, but youngsters without the use of their legs can use their arms or drive underwater 'scooters'. The real problem is getting into and out of the water. The solution is a boat that's equipped with an electrically or hydraulically powered lift platform, as increasing numbers of the better boats are.

The deaf and dumb could even be said to be at an advantage underwater. While able-bodied divers are normally restricted to a very limited number of hand signals, the deaf and dumb can continue their full conversations as normal.

We've already covered diving for the able-bodied in Chapter 3 so take a look at that for general information.

Specifically where those with disabilities are concerned, the Scuba Trust (**www.scubatrust.org.uk** Tel: 07985 025 385) is a good place to start. It runs monthly 'introduction to diving' sessions which let both disabled and able-bodied family members see how they get on. If you all like it, you might like to consider a holiday run by the trust.

As one disabled diver put it: "I dive and many of my able-bodied friends can't even do that."

If diving doesn't appeal, or there are practical reasons why the equipment can't be used, you may still find that snorkelling is possible.

### FURTHER INFORMATION

For further information on disabled diving take a look at **www.ifyoudive.com**, **www.divewise.com**, **www.iahd.org** and **www.hsascuba.com**.

## Some questions to ask

✓ Where will initial training be carried out?

✓ Does everyone speak English?

✓ What facilities does the boat have for disabled children?

✓ How will my disabled child be got into the water?

✓ How will my disabled child be recovered from the water?

✓ How many professional staff will be supervising the diving?

✓ Does the dive boat carry oxygen?

✓ Where is the nearest decompression chamber?

## Why is this good for families with disabled children?

In the 'weightless' undersea world everyone becomes more equal.

## Pros

● The chance to experience a degree of mobility which may be impossible on land.

## Cons

● Disability is an additional hazard in a potentially dangerous environment.

## Where to go

The Scuba Trust runs diving holidays for the disabled in Spain.

## When

Summer.

## Price Guide

'Try Dives' with the Scuba Trust cost £20 while a full 'open water' course is £350.

# Unusual Family Holiday (Including Children With Disabilities) No. 56: Skiing

Like diving, skiing might seem to be one of the last things anyone with a disability should attempt on holiday. But skiing can provide exactly that exhilaration in movement that so many disabled children have lost. In fact, the charity Disability Snowsport UK avows that 'anyone, regardless of their disability, can take part.' That's their mission.

We often ski at Les Angles in the French Pyrenees where the ski station makes a special effort to welcome disabled children. Usually they're on what are known as mono-skis and having a wonderful time. But there are several options:

*Mono-ski:* a seat mounted on a single ski and controlled with the help of hand held outriggers (forearm crutches with miniature skis at the base). The mono-ski is specially designed to interlock with the chair-lift, allowing a child to ride up and ski down with the minimum of assistance.

*Bi-ski:* a seat mounted on two skis and requiring less skill and strength.

*Three-track:* for children who have lost a leg, or the use of a leg, this set-up consists of one ski and two outriggers.

*Four-track:* for children who have the use of both legs but have problems of balance and control, this consists of two skis and two outriggers.

*Bi-ski + helper:* for children who can't cope with any of those options, a bi-ski can be controlled by another skier.

*Radio link:* blind skiers are led down by a sighted companion giving instructions transmitted to an earpiece.

With all these possibilities, the vast majority of children with disabilities can get onto the slopes and experience the thrill of carving turns using gravity and the curve of the mountains.

Skiers with disabilities are just like other skiers. Some go slowly down the easiest runs and others go fast down difficult runs. Sometimes very fast. If you have a disabled child there's no reason you can't all fully enjoy your skiing together. It isn't a question of able-bodied and disabled, just of the standard of skiing. There's no reason everybody can't have a great time.

But, obviously, you're not going to find the necessary equipment for hire in every resort. The best thing is to go with a specialist company or charity that has the equipment, knows the most suitable resorts and has made arrangements with the lift operating company.

## FURTHER INFORMATION

For general information on winter sports see the next chapter.

### Some specialist operators

**www.bscd.org.uk** Tel: 01869 327 445 – British Ski Club for the Disabled (BSCD).

**www.redpoint.co.uk** Tel: 01902 568 034

**www.disabilitysnowsport.org.uk** Tel: 01479 861 272

**www.excite.co.uk** – directory; follow links for disability related sites.

**www.adaptiveski.org** (New Mexico, USA) 00 1 505 995 9858

**www.challengemtn.org** (USA) Tel: 00 1 231 535 2141

**www.loisirs-assis-evasion.com** (France) Tel: 00 33 67 339 8178

**www.handiconcept.com** (Switzerland) Tel: 00 41 792 407 082

### Some questions to ask

✓ Are you specialists in skiing for the disabled?

✓ Do you have all the necessary equipment?

✓ Is the resort sympathetic to disabled skiers?

✓ Are the resort staff trained to assist disabled skiers?

✓ What other facilities in the resort are accessible to the disabled?

✓ Will the resort streets be clear of snow?

### Why is this good for families with disabled children?

With the right equipment, the piste can put a child with disabilities on the same level as everyone else in the family.

### Pros

● Healthy exercise for everyone.

### Cons

● Just getting around in ski resorts can be difficult for the able-bodied, let alone anyone with disabilities.

### Where to go

Les Angles, French Pyrenees; Chamonix, Morzine, Megève and St Gervais in the French Alps; Villars in Switzerland; the Sierra Nevada in Spain;

Redpoint organises skiing for the disabled in Austria's Ziller Valley. Many USA resorts. Try putting your favoured resort into your search engine and then follow links for disabled facilities.

## When

March/April — it's easier in sunny weather when the snow has melted in the village.

## Price guide

Several US resorts offer three hour lessons with all equipment and lift pass for around £50. A full day's bi-ski with helper costs around £250 with Switzerland's Handiconcept. A week's skiing with Assis Evasion costs from £650 including accommodation. Disabled skiers can tackle the famous Vallée Blanche off-piste itinerary at Chamonix for around £130.

# Unusual Family Holiday (Including Children With Disabilities) No. 57: Animal Assisted Therapy

We're great fans of something that's called Animal Assisted Therapy (AAT). We've experienced and seen some of the benefits for ourselves and we're totally persuaded. As a holiday, AAT can help children (and adults) with a range of disabilities while at the same time providing other members of the family with a thrilling and unforgettable experience. All kinds of animals can be used including cats and dogs but in a holiday context it's normally dolphins and horses.

*

Swimming with dolphins (see Chapter 1) is such a wonderful experience that it certainly shouldn't be confined to the able-bodied. On the contrary, it's often children with special needs who benefit the most.

Let's try to put the power of dolphins into perspective. Nobody is claiming that dolphins can magically cure human disorders. But they can certainly bring about a substantial improvement in certain mental health problems such as depression. And there are many parents who say that dolphins had more impact on certain physical problems than conventional treatments did.

The idea that swimming with dolphins could have therapeutic effects goes back to at least the 1950s and the work of Dr John Lilly. More recently, Dr Horace Dobbs (**www.horacedobbs.com**), founder of International Dolphin Watch (**www.idw.org**), has done a huge amount to promote the concept.

Some scientists have theorised that dolphins might be able to target exquisitely fine sonar beams into different parts of the human body. Another suggestion is that a dolphin's energy field might interact with human energy fields. What is sure is that dolphins fill almost everyone with a sense of exhilaration and joy.

The easiest and cheapest way to interact is at dolphin amusement parks and some, indeed, do offer therapy. But there are ethical considerations. Dolphins are highly intelligent creatures with minds we do not understand and shouldn't be confined in that way. The Born Free Foundation believes people should not swim with captive dolphins and we support that view. What's more, many therapists believe that interaction with free dolphins in their natural environment is far more powerful than anything in a swimming pool. But exactly how do you set about finding dolphins in the vastness of the oceans?

Well, in fact, there are dolphins that either stay permanently in an area or at least, like migrating birds, return to a specific spot at certain times of the year. One such location is Bimini in the Bahamas, a short trip from Miami, where a pod is resident and used to human contact. Operation Sunshine, a not for profit organisation which comes under the umbrella of International Dolphin Watch, organises trips to interact with these dolphins.

Operating in the Gulf of Mexico, Wild And Free says it can help children with autism, depression, cystic fibrosis, cerebral palsy, spina bifida, muscular dystrophy and many other disorders. Dolphin encounters take place in the mornings in the waters just off Panama City, northwestern Florida, while afternoons are the time for complementary work including hydrotherapy, massage, Watsu (water shiatsu), cranio sacral therapy, and art and music workshops.

All the family can take part in these encounters. But the problem with wild dolphin therapy is that it's a very expensive business which necessarily has to take place in waters far warmer than we have in the UK. Unless you're exceedingly wealthy it's a 'once in a lifetime' kind of thing whereas children with special needs really require frequent interactions. Horses are a different but much more affordable option.

*

Happy turned out to be the most inappropriate name we could have chosen for a new foal. By the age of five, after various trainers and experts had been flung to the ground, we gave up on him. Until one day a man in a cowboy hat turned up and said he'd like to buy Happy.

Impossible, we said. He's so nervous that he's dangerous. The man insisted. He liked horses with problems. And he needed a strong, black pony. And that's how it was we gave Happy to the Rainbow Ranch where, in the years since, Happy has helped dozens of youngsters overcome the most severe kinds of psychological trauma.

What happens at the Rainbow Ranch, which is based in the Costa Brava region of Spain, is known as equitherapy. Youngsters (and adults, too) select a horse to work with during their stay and, inevitably, they choose a horse that has the same problem they do themselves. That's why the cowboy had been so keen to have a pony that lived in an almost constant state of terror.

It works in two ways. Firstly, the psychologist can watch the reactions provoked by the chosen horse and learn things that might never have come out in the consulting room. Secondly, something often happens *between* the horse and the client, something almost magical, that changes the traumatised youngster's view of the world. We've seen for ourselves how effective it can be. And it's not just individuals who can be helped. A child's disability – perhaps caused by an accident – may cause trauma for the whole family. Equitherapy can help mend those relationships.

Of course, the horse can't do everything on its own. The quality of the experience also depends very much on the handler and the psychologist.

Rainbow Ranch was one of the first outside the USA, where equitherapy began, and there are still only a dozen or so centres in the UK and Europe. But the number is growing all the time as therapists become trained in the technique. Only some equitherapy centres cater for family problems and only some have holiday riding facilities for family members not taking part in the programme, so you'll need to discuss your requirements very carefully. In certain cases you'll have to be referred by a psychologist.

*

Equitherapy is for mental health problems but horses are more widely used for physical problems. It all goes back to the 1952 Helsinki Olympics at which Liz Hartel won a silver medal in equestrian sports and ascribed her recovery from polio to riding. Since then techniques have been developed to help children with a range of conditions including cerebral palsy, autism, Asperger Syndrome, Down's Syndrome and brain injury.

Horses seem to notice when children have disabilities. They adapt their movements and behaviour accordingly. And, in fact, children with disabilities often establish a greater rapport with their ponies and horses than other children and adults. It could simply be that the animals feel less under threat.

Lee Pearson who suffers from arthrogryphosis multiplex congenita won three gold medals for riding at Sydney 2000 and says he would "urge anyone – able-bodied or disabled – to give it a go." Horses, he explains, "give you the freedom, movement and energy" that operating a wheelchair just can't.

When a child with disabilities sits on a horse mostly for pleasure it's known as 'therapeutic riding' but when riding is specifically used as a treatment it's known as 'hippotherapy'. The key is the constant, rhythmic movement of the horse which manipulates the pelvis almost as if the rider were walking. Being on a horse develops balance and exercises and trains the muscles. The intensity of the input is controlled by the therapist, telling the horse either to go faster or slower.

## FURTHER INFORMATION

To learn more about dolphin therapy read Horace Dobbs' *Journey Into Dolphin Dreamtime* (Jonathan Cape, 1992). To learn more about equitherapy and for a list of equitherapy centres contact the Equine Assisted Growth And Learning Association **www.eagala.org.uk**

### Some specialist operators

### Dolphin therapy

**www.operationsunshine.org** – charity for bringing dolphins together with people who need their help.

**www.wild-and-free.co.uk** Tel: 0845 345 9052 – UK contact for Florida based operation.

**www.dolphinhumantherapy.com** Tel: 00 1 305 378 8670 Miami and Key Largo, Florida.

### Equitherapy

**www.windsofchangescotland.co.uk** Tel: 01349 877 560 Dingwall, Scotland.

**www.gentleleadership.com** Tel: 01339 755 954 Ballater, Scotland.

**www.halona.co.uk** Tel: 01697 741 292 Armathwaite, Cumbria.
**www.halter.org.uk** Tel: 01274 784 976 Bradford.
**www.rainbowranch.nl** Tel: 00 34 690 288 624 Spain.

## Riding for the disabled (Hippotherapy)

**www.riding-for-the-disabled.org.uk** Tel: 0845 658 1082
**www.frdi.net** Federation of Riding for the Disabled International.

## Some questions to ask

✓ What kind of disabilities does this therapy cater for?

✓ What kind of benefits can be expected?

✓ Is there any risk?

✓ Can the whole family enjoy this experience?

✓ What qualifications do you have?

✓ How long have you been doing this kind of work?

✓ What insurance will we need?

## Why is this good for families with disabled children?

Meaningful, structured contact with animals is wonderful for everyone. Horse riding, in particular, can be a great leveller, allowing able-bodied and disabled to ride together and enjoy themselves – it's the horse, after all, that does most of the work.

## Pros

- A holiday and treatment all rolled into one.

## Cons

- Where treatment is the main focus, holiday facilities for the able-bodied may not be well thought out.

## Where to go

Dolphin therapy needs warm water and resident dolphins – Florida (and the Caribbean) are good. Equitherapy and hippotherapy centres exist in the UK and many popular holiday destinations including France, Spain, Portugal and the USA.

## When

Riding is best spring to autumn in the UK but with a covered school it's possible year round; in southern Europe avoid the summer with its heat and flies. Dolphin encounters: summer.

## Price Guide

Wild dolphin therapy is extremely expensive. Think in terms of £700 for a disabled child, £550 for an able-bodied brother or sister and £400 for each accompanying adult. That's not including flights or accommodation. Equitherapy is significantly cheaper and can cost from around £75 per session, again not including transport or accommodation; several sessions will be necessary.

# Unusual Family Holiday (Including Children With Disabilities) No. 58: Sailing

Sailing has a magic that everyone can respond to, irrespective of disability. There's something about the way a sailing boat heels, something about the curve of the sails, something about the sound of the spray hitting the foredeck, even something about the gentle, rhythmic movement of the boat in the harbour that connects us with the life giving forces of the universe.

At first sight a sailing boat doesn't seem to provide a suitable environment for a disabled child – all those ropes, the flapping sails, the narrow, slippery side decks and the crazy angle, to say nothing of the salt spray down the neck. But some marvellous people in both the charitable and commercial sectors have devised a whole range of adaptations that make it possible for children with disabilities to get onto boats, enjoy the thrills and even take part in all the tasks such as hauling up sails and steering.

The Jubilee Sailing Trust owns and operates two tall ships, the Lord Nelson and the Tenacious, both based at Southampton but also operating out of other ports including London and Edinburgh. They are the only tall ships in the world specially designed to enable the physically disabled and able-bodied to work together on equal terms, making them perfect for families with a disabled child. For the sight impaired, for example, there's a speaking compass while for those confined to wheelchairs (they mustn't be electric) there are lifts between the decks. With a permanent crew of 10, no previous sailing experience is necessary. But even so every passenger has to help run the ship and work four hours on duty followed by 12 hours off. Voyages last for anything from a day (minimum age 12) up to a transatlantic crossing (minimum age 16) **www.jst.org.uk** Tel: 023 8044 9138.

DR Yachting is a commercial company offering sailing holidays in the Greek islands. Adaptations to the boats have been carefully thought through. For boarding, for example, there are 90cm wide gangways, there are seatbelts on all seats and handles placed to make moving around safe and secure. Solis Invictis can carry eight passengers, of whom two can be in wheelchairs. It's possible to charter the entire boat, with a skipper and hostess, or simply to book a cabin for two **www.disabledsailingholidays.com** Tel: 00 30 210 985 0168/9.

Bournemouth Sports Forum for the Disabled operates a Catalac sailing catamaran which has been adapted to allow winches and sheets (ropes) to be worked from a wheelchair in the cockpit. The catamaran – the Knoticat – is based at Poole and sails the Solent area during the summer. There is no charge for disabled people and their carers although the charity points out that 'donations are always welcome' **www. disabled.sports.btinternet.co.uk/newsailingpage.htm** Tel: 01202 520 249.

Various sailing charities offer facilities for disabled youngsters on their own. The Rona Trust, for example, particularly helps the visually impaired and deaf and has three yachts based on the River Hamble, sailing along the south coast and to France **www.ronatrust.com** Tel: 01489 885 098.

If there's one name in sailing that's associated with true grit it's that of Ellen MacArthur. The Ellen MacArthur Trust, set up in 2003, is specifically for children suffering from cancer or leukaemia **www.ellenmacarthurtrust.org** Tel: 0870 063 6774. The trust operates various yachts based at Cowes on the Isle of Wight ranging from 12m to 14m and the children normally stay away for several days, sleeping in a different port each night.

## FURTHER INFORMATION

For a full list of sailing organisations that have facilities for the disabled see **www.asto.org.uk**. There's a useful forum for sailors with disabilities at **www.disabledsailing.org.uk**. The Royal Yachting Association operates a scheme known as Sailability to help sailing clubs develop facilities for the disabled **www.rya.org.uk/sailability** Tel: 0845 345 0403.

### Some questions to ask

✓ What kind of disabilities are your boats equipped for?

✓ Can we come as a family with a disabled child?

✓ Is there a facility for getting a disabled child into and out of the water for swimming?

✓ How can a disabled child get ashore during the trip?

✓ Is any previous sailing experience necessary?

✓ How many professional crew will there be?

✓ What would we be expected to do?

✓ Is there any risk?

✓ What qualifications do the crew have?

✓ What insurance will we need?

## Why is this good for families with disabled children?

Every member of the family can play a role in sailing the boat and equally enjoy the pleasures of sailing.

### Pros

• Builds confidence.

### Cons

• Seasickness.

• The sea can be a very demanding environment, especially around Britain.

### Where to go

Anywhere there's water, but the Greek Islands are always a good bet.

### When

Summer.

### Price Guide

There are some wonderful charities and people providing disabled children and their carers with the experience of sailing very cheaply or even free of charge. But operating sailing boats is an expensive business and, at the other extreme, prices can be over £1,000 a week each. A day trip on one of the tall ships costs £125 each (including food) while a transatlantic crossing would be £1,250.

# And finally

If you want more activities...

The Calvert Trust has been providing outdoor activities for people with disabilities for 20 years, including canoeing, kayaking, climbing, riding and archery. The trust operates centres at Exmoor, Keswick and Kielder with accommodation accessible to wheelchair users. Holidays cost from around £265 up to £395 a week, including the activities **www.calvert-trust.org.uk** Tel: Exmoor 01598 763 221; Keswick 01768 772 255; Kielder 01434 250 232.

If you just want to take it easy...

The pleasures of historic buildings with their narrow corridors and creaking staircases just aren't accessible to those with disabilities. So it's wonderful to find a 200 year old Spanish *finca* that's been renovated specifically with the needs of disabled people in mind, including wheelchair access to the terraces and swimming pool. The *finca* is in the traditional village of Finestrat, near Benidorm **www.oasis-holiday.com** Tel: 01892 665 294 (UK) or 00 34 965 878 629 (Spain).

# Chapter 14

# Winter Sports Holidays

**Unusual family holidays in this chapter: downhill skiing, snowboarding, cross country skiing, snowshoeing, dog mushing and much more.**

Just as the beach is the obvious place for a family in summer, so a snow covered mountain is the obvious place in winter. Believe us! For swimming read skiing. For surfing read snowboarding. For deckchair on the sand read deckchair on the snow. For *taverna* on the beach read mountain restaurant. For squid and chips read fondue. For all over tan read face and hands. For discotheque read, er, discotheque. And in some resorts you might even get a decent outdoor swim (highly recommended for the curious experience of being in steaming warm water whilst surrounded by snow).

In some families, everybody turns into a mad keen skier. But if you don't think that's going to be the case with your family then you need one of the larger resorts offering such additional diversions as spas, beauty treatments, saunas, shops, casinos, bowling alleys, bars, restaurants, discos, sleigh rides, trips out to the surrounding area, swimming, snowboarding, cross country skiing, skating, curling, snow shoeing, paragliding, riding and dog mushing.

The more sharp eyed among you will have noticed a lot of physical activities in the list. And in the interests of accuracy it has to be said that members of the family who aren't interested in any activities whatsoever at all, even a little bit, are going to be, well, *bored*. But everybody else is going to have a great time.

Downhill skiing and snowboarding are the mainstays of most families' winter sports holidays. Other activities are thrown in now and then just for a change. But, for convenience, we're describing each of the main activities as a holiday in its own right.

# Unusual Family Holiday No. 59: Downhill Skiing

There's a certain amount of luck involved in a successful first family ski holiday. You need luck with the weather (snow at night, sunny all day) and luck with the people who are looking after and teaching your children. But when it goes well nothing can beat it.

In many resorts you'll see children as young as three bombing down the runs. But don't be fooled. Those are local children who have long been exposed to snow culture. In one or two weeks you can't expect your three year old from Flatland to do the same or even attempt it. Six is probably the earliest age you can expect a child from the plains to get interested. Send your kids to ski kindergarten or junior ski school, depending on age, and let the professionals deal with it. The kids will soon make friends and falling over isn't half so bad when everybody else is doing it, too.

And while we're on the subject, you get along to ski school as well. Don't go thinking that lessons are no longer necessary just because today's equipment is so much easier than the long, wooden planks of 50 years ago. If you want to make any progress then professional lessons are the way to do it.

Oh, and if you're already a competent skier think twice before giving lessons to other family members or friends. We've made the mistake more than once and we've got a lot fewer friends than we used to have.

If you're the adult in the party who just isn't very physical then don't worry. For you they invented short skis – skis that have been shrunk to anything between 90cm and 135cm. You won't be able to go very fast but you will be able to turn with just a couple of hours' tuition. (Remember that ski length is relative to height, weight and experience and a 90cm ski that's short for an adult is *not* short for a child. Don't put children on short adult skis. Get them properly fitted out in a specialist ski rental outlet with skis specifically suitable for them.)

An alternative to each of you going along to your own class is to book private tuition for all of you together as a family. The fact that you're not all at the same level doesn't mean you can't tackle the same runs. You'll just do them in your own different ways. You'll learn in a shorter time and if there are four of you or more then your private group lesson should compare favourably with regular ski school.

So how quickly can you expect to be whooshing down the slopes as a family? You could be doing long green and blue runs (the two easiest grades) on your second day. And by the end of the week you should be doing reds (the next rank). But it's probably best to leave the black runs (the hardest) to your second week or second holiday.

## FURTHER INFORMATION

For general information the Ski Club of Great Britain is a good place to start **www.skiclub.co.uk**; also take a look at **www.onthesnow.com** and **www.ski-holidays.com**. For the low-down on all the world's major resorts buy *Where To Ski And Snowboard* (NortonWood) which is updated every year. You can rent equipment in the ski resort or in advance through your tour operator or try **www.snowrental.net**.

### Some specialist operators

**www.crystalski.co.uk** Tel: 0870 160 6040

**www.ernalow.co.uk** Tel: 0870 750 6820

**www.neilson.co.uk** Tel: 0870 333 3356

**www.inghams.co.uk** Tel: 020 8780 4433

**www.thomsonski.com** Tel: 0870 888 0254

**www.firstchoice.co.uk/ski** Tel: 0870 850 3999

**www.ifyouski.com** Tel: (chalets) 0870 043 5305; (hotels) 0870 043 5306; (apartments) 0870 739 9399

**www.igluski.com** Tel: 020 8544 6413

**www.ski-direct.co.uk** Tel: 0870 0171 935

**www.skimcneill.com** Tel: 0870 600 1359

**www.alpine-tracks.co.uk** Tel: 0800 028 2546

### Some chalet specialists

**www.chaletfinder.co.uk** Tel: 01453 766 094

**www.skichalets.co.uk** Tel: 01202 503 950

**www.chaletworldski.co.uk** Tel: 01743 231 199

### Some specialist travel agencies

**www.skisolutions.com** Tel: 020 7471 7700

**www.alpineanswers.co.uk** Tel: 020 8871 4656

**www.snowfinders.com** Tel: 0858 466 888

**www.skimcneill.com** Tel: 0870 600 1359

## Some questions to ask

✓ Is there a kindergarten with qualified English speaking staff?

✓ Is there an English speaking ski school that's good with children?

✓ Are the children's nursery slopes near the 'adult' slopes?

✓ What other activities are there?

✓ What non-skiing activities are there?

✓ Is this resort suitable for our level (beginner/intermediate/advanced)?

✓ Is the snow reliable?

✓ What's the altitude of the resort? Of the top lift?

✓ Are there plenty of modern, high speed chairlifts, gondolas and cable cars?

✓ Does the resort offer sufficient variety for a 1 week/2 week holiday?

✓ Is it crowded?

✓ Can we easily ski other resorts in the area if we want a change?

✓ What insurance should we have?

✓ What's the nightlife like?

## Why is this good for families?

If everybody takes to skiing then it's one of the most exhilarating ways you can spend quality time together.

## Pros

• An invigorating getaway when British weather is at its worst.

## Cons

• If there's a cold snap, or days when it snows, it's a tough environment for young children. The cost of travel and accommodation is only the start of it all; there are also ski hire, lifts and lessons to pay for.

## Where to go

Modern, purpose built resorts are efficient but they just don't have much atmosphere. Where children are concerned it's hard to beat the 'fairy tale' villages in Austria and Switzerland. And there are a few in Italy, too. The French Alps boast good lift systems but very little charm, except for Châtel, Les Contamines, Les Gets, La Grave, Megève, Puy-St-Vincent, Samoëns and St-Martin-de-Belleville. The Pyrenees (France, Spain and Andorra) have smaller resorts and less development but good ski touring. Don't bother with Scotland unless you live there. California combines sunshine with a long season and lessons guaranteed to be in English.

## Ski resorts especially good for children

Arinsal and Soldeu in Andorra, for their English speaking instructors; Avoriaz, Flaine, Morzine, La Plagne, Puy-St-Vincent, Risoul, Les Sybelles and Valmorel in France for their nurseries and child friendly ski schools; Alpbach, Bad Gastein, Ellmau, Seefeld and Westendorf in Austria for child friendly everything; Adelboden, Grindelwald, Saas-Fee and Verbier in Switzerland for the same reason; Heavenly and Mammoth in California.

## When

For young children it's important to have long, warm, sunny days, but the February half-term will be horribly crowded. March/early April is probably best. In the highest resorts the season generally opens at the beginning of December and finishes at the beginning of May (slightly later at Mammoth, California). But in the lower resorts it's much shorter. Given the unreliability of snow it makes sense to watch the snow reports and make a last minute booking. If booking ahead go for the highest resorts and, unless you like crowds, avoid Christmas to New Year and most of February.

## Price guide

A week's ski holiday in Europe costs from around £300 self-catering with flight, up to around £1,000 full board in a good hotel. You can go to California from around £600 for a week (flight + B&B). On top of that you'll have to pay per week: £45–£100 for equipment hire; £80–£150 (£25 for cross country) for a ski pass; £75 for two hours ski school per day. The low season will be significantly cheaper than the high season (Christmas/New Year, February and Easter if it's early). Expect to pay around £200 extra for day long childcare.

## Saving Money

Winter sports holidays can be extremely expensive for families so here are some ideas for cuttings costs.

**Late booking:** If you don't mind too much where you go you might snap up a last minute deal. And you won't have to take a chance on the snow.

**The DIY approach:** Book an apartment direct on the internet and you could be talking in terms of as little as £65 each for the week. Flights on a low cost airline could be about the same. Hire a car for transfers and for shopping down in the valley where the prices will be cheaper.

**Ski clothing:** Anything you buy for the kids this season won't fit next season so why not hire? You can kit out a child for around £40–£75 for a week's skiing (and you get a few extra days for collecting and returning). Check with your nearest specialist shop to see if they rent clothing; two that do are **www.skitogshire.co.uk** Tel: 020 8993 9883 (London) and 01993 700 223 (Whitney). If you're going to buy, you might find bargains in pre-season sales; if you're skiing late (say, April) you might also do well in end of season sales.

**Lift passes:** The policy on discounts varies from resort to resort so it's worth checking. The resorts of the Italian 'Milky Way', for example, including Sauze d'Oulx and Sestriere, offer free six day passes to children under 10; Obergurgl and Zermatt do the same for under nines.

**Low season:** The low season not only means low prices but smaller lift queues. Try just before Christmas, mid-January and April – but watch the snow reports.

## Unusual Family Holiday No. 60: Snowboarding

If your kids are already into skateboarding they'll take to snowboarding like the proverbial ducks to water. But if none of you have done anything like it before how do you decide: skis or snowboards?

Well, the difference between skis and snowboards can be summarised like this: snowboards are harder at first but much easier later. And it's not difficult to see why. When you've got your feet on two separate skis it's much simpler to get your balance than when both feet are strapped to the same plank. So on a snowboard you tend to fall over a lot at first. And it *hurts*. For that reason many ski schools have a minimum age of eight for learning snowboard.

But fast forward to the end of the week and things look rather different. The snowboarders are going to be coming down harder runs, faster and with more style. Quite simply, there's a knack to a snowboard and once you've got it you've learned 90 per cent of everything necessary. Skis are just much more complicated.

A few other practical considerations. It's much harder to get up a drag lift (ie you stand and get dragged up) on a snowboard than it is on skis, so if your resort doesn't have plenty of modern chair lifts and cable cars you're in for a frustrating time on a board. Secondly, there are things called terrain parks. They're places where the snow has been shaped into all kinds of things like jumps and U-shaped descents called half-pipes. They're the snowy equivalent of the places skateboarders hang out in city centres. Those in the family who like that culture should opt for snowboards. It's true you can also do tricks on skis but it's much harder.

Apart from that, it's just a question of personal taste and style. Forget the notion that snowboards are for youngsters and skis for oldsters. That's all changed. You'll see 70 year olds on snowboards – so bring the grandparents, too.

The final thing to point out is that boarding comes in two styles – hard boots and soft boots. Hard boots ('alpine' style) are for fast cruising and nothing more. Soft boots are more manoeuvrable. Unless you're positive that alpine style is what you want, go for soft boots.

### Safety tip

Make sure your children wear helmets and wrist protectors – and do the same yourself. There's no fashion problem – helmets are considered cool as well as being practical. It's not just a question of the speed you're going, it's also about the speed of the person who hits you.

### Why is this good for families?

A snowboard is a great vehicle for self-expression, which means all the family can enjoy themselves in their own different ways. Youngsters can hang out in the terrain park learning tricks while older members of the family can cruise the mountain and make long stops to drink hot chocolate.

### Pros

- It's easier to get good on a snowboard than it is on skis.
- Snowboards are cool.

## Cons

- You fall over a lot at first and it *hurts*.

## Where to go

The same places as for skiing (above) except (a) avoid resorts with lots of tricky drag lifts and (b) check that there's a terrain park — a boarder's playground.

## When

As for skiing.

## Price guide

As for skiing.

## Learn Before You Go

Britain now has four indoor slopes with real snow — Glasgow, Leeds, Milton Keynes and Tamworth. Even the longest (Glasgow) is a mere 200m, but that's quite enough to learn and to get fit. You'll have to pay around £22 an hour for adults and around £15 an hour for children (the same as you'd pay for a whole *day* in some Alpine and Pyrenean resorts) but look upon it as an investment — you'll get more out of your holiday as a result **www.xscape.co.uk** and **www.snowdome.co.uk**.

Snowboarders can get fit and practise on open hillsides with mountainboards — large skateboards with chunky off-road wheels **www.sw-mbc.co.uk** Tel: 07866 398 599.

## My Children Are Too Young To Ski

No matter how much he protests he won't, dad inevitably succumbs to the temptation of those curvaceous slopes and leaves mum with the non-skiing kids. The rotter! Of course, almost all resorts have nurseries but the standard is pretty variable as are English skills. So any company that can more or less guarantee the kids will be well looked after should make money and save quite a few marriages. Esprit Ski is such a company. It offers around 150 properties in Austria, France, Italy and Switzerland. At 8.30 each morning the children are whisked away to nursery, ski lessons or snow club as appropriate and parents don't collect them until around 5pm. Seven night packages for a family of four cost from around £1,500 including childcare and children's ski lessons.

**www.esprit-holidays.co.uk** Tel: 01252 618 300

Other family friendly operators include:

**www.skifamille.co.uk** Tel: 0845 644 3764

**www.powderbyrne.co.uk** Tel: 020 8246 5300

**www.scottdunn.com** Tel: 020 8682 5050

**www.markwarner.co.uk** Tel: 0870 770 4228

## Unusual Family Holiday No. 61: Cross Country Skiing And Snowshoeing

A lot of people love the mountains in winter but hate the crowds on the pistes, the ugly lifts and the music that some resorts play. If you want mountains, snow *and* tranquillity then you need either cross country skis or snow shoes so you can get away into the woods and even the wilderness.

To be frank, tranquillity isn't something most kids are too bothered about. But if yours are, or they've reached that age when the finer things in life have begun to appeal, then this could be perfect.

When you've all got your snowshoes on you're essentially walking. So you don't need much skill although, once you start to go uphill, you'll certainly need plenty of endurance. A couple of ski poles can help. Look for large snowshoes in plastic with a quick and secure method of attachment – there's nothing more annoying than straps constantly working loose. For steeper work a heel lift is desirable. And a built-in crampon.

When you click your feet into cross country skis, on the other hand, you can walk and run *and glide*. So you can cover the ground much faster, usually on specially prepared trails. You won't face the kind of slopes you would for downhill skiing but the hills that there are do require a certain amount of skill. So everyone is going to need a lesson or two.

### FURTHER INFORMATION

#### Some questions to ask

How many kilometres of cross country trails/snow shoe paths are there?

What grades?

Is the snow reliable? (Cross country trails are usually in the valley bottom where the snow *isn't* reliable.)

Is tuition available in English?

## Why is this good for families?

Some routes are harder than others (and marked accordingly) but, generally, there's none of the fear that you get in snowboarding and downhill skiing. Everybody should be able to do it (although not at the same speed).

## Pros

• No expensive lift passes, no crowds, no dangerous falls.

## Cons

• Hard work and none of the exhilarating speed of downhill skiing. If your kids don't like hiking they probably won't like this, either.

## Where to go

Most ski resorts have at least some cross country trails but if you want to make this the focus of your holiday try: Seefeld (Austria); Alpe'd'Huez, Avoriaz, La Clusaz, Megève, Méribel, Morzine, La Plagne, Puy-St-Vincent, St-Martin-de-Belleville, La Toussuire, La Tania and Tignes (France); Cortina d'Ampezzo, Courmayeur, Livigno, Madonna di Campiglio, Monterosa and Selva (Italy); Heavenly and Mammoth (California).

## When

Cross country trails tend to be at lower altitude than downhill *pistes* so aim for February in Europe, the most reliable snow month. Or book at the last minute when you know where the snow is.

## Price guide

The same as for skiing except you won't need a lift pass. The equipment is cheaper to purchase/hire, too.

# Unusual Family Holiday No. 62: Ski Touring

If you already can all ski (or snowboard) to a good standard then skiing *real* snow is one of the most ravishing things you can do. There's nothing like the shared effort of climbing up to a ridge followed by the exhilaration of a descent through virgin powder to bring about a little family bonding. Isn't it dangerous? Not necessarily. After all, before the invention of lifts *everybody* had to climb up the hard way. It's all a question of choosing suitable routes.

The first step is to get back to ski school and either join a class in off-piste technique (it's quite different) or hire a guide to give you lessons as a family. You'll probably begin by taking the usual lifts but descending through the deep snow at the side of the piste. But once you get to the stage where you want to climb up away from the ski lifts then, unfortunately, you're going to need extra equipment, including special skis that allow you to hike up as well as ski down. Which, whether you rent or buy, means more money.

Anyone who snowboards is going to find the transition to real snow much easier. The drawback – once you get away from the lifts - is that you have to carry the board up on a backpack while wearing snow shoes. Not something many youngsters are up to or would relish. A split board provides a rather brilliant solution – it divides into two 'skis' for the hike up and is reassembled for the descent. But not many equipment shops have them at the moment.

---

### AVALANCHES

The big danger off-piste is the avalanche. Resorts work tirelessly to keep their runs safe (by blowing up unstable cornices, for example) but there's nobody to do that in the wilderness. The number one golden rule is never to ski off-piste when the snow reports say the danger is high. You'd not just endanger your own life but also the lives of everybody below you. The second golden rule is to hire a guide.

---

## FURTHER INFORMATION

For general information about ski touring take a look at **www.eagleskiclub.org.uk**; for links to specialist operators see **www.travel-quest.co.uk**.

### Some specialist operators

**www.alpine-guides.com** Tel: 07940 407 533

**www.mountaintracks.co.uk** Tel: 020 8877 5773

**www.peakretreats.co.uk** Tel: 0870 770 0408

**www.alpineadventures.co.uk** Tel: 00 33 45 054 7344

**www.mountainbug.com** Tel: 00 33 56 292 1639

**www.responsibletravel.com** Tel: 01273 600 030

## Some questions to ask

✓ Are there off-piste itineraries suitable for youngsters?

✓ Will children have to carry anything?

✓ How much ascent will we be doing?

✓ How hard are the descents?

✓ Are there any lifts we can use?

✓ What happens if there's an accident?

✓ What qualifications do your guides have?

✓ Are you fully equipped for avalanches (avalanche transceivers, probes, shovels)?

✓ What insurance do we need?

## Why is this good for families?

Getting out in the mountains together is both a physical and spiritual experience.

## Pros

● No crowds.

● Close to nature.

## Cons

● It's very hard work and probably won't appeal under the age of 14.

● There's always the risk of injury – or even death.

## Where to go

Where youngsters are concerned the Pyrenees are best – the terrain is relatively easy, serious avalanches are few and the weather is kinder.

## When

It's best to go when there's plenty of daylight – that's to say, later in the season when days are longer. Say March/April. *Never* go when there's a high risk of avalanche.

## Price guide

For four days off-piste expect to pay £350–£700 depending on season, including the guide and half-board accommodation but not including flights, lifts or equipment hire. For six days coaching expect to pay £745.

## Unusual Family Holiday No. 63: Dog Mushing

Almost all children love dog mushing, even if they hate every other winter sport. What could be more wonderful than cuddly dogs pulling you on a sleigh? And the dogs love it too. No doubt about that. Their joyful gambolling and howling sets up an electricity that's infectious. It's almost impossible not to have a good time.

Even the youngest children can take part, although in their case they'll have to ride as passengers inside the sledge. Adults and older children can drive their own teams, standing on the runners at the back and operating a foot brake when needed. It isn't necessary to have much skill because the dogs all follow the guide. How hard it is depends on the terrain. Ideally you want flat snow (a frozen lake is perfect) or gently rolling landscape. Traversing steepish slopes is, frankly, only for strong teenagers and fit adults.

Sadly, running dog teams is a pretty expensive business so only the uber wealthy could afford to make a whole holiday of it. On the other hand, an hour would probably be the highlight of the holiday for a six year old, as would a half-day for teenagers and adults.

Not everybody uses the traditional huskies because, although gentle with humans, they still answer all too readily to the call of the wild or the neighbour's chickens. But there's no doubt that with their gorgeous fur and laughing mouths they really make the experience.

### FURTHER INFORMATION

#### Some specialist operators

Not all operators allow you to drive your own team so check carefully what's on offer.

**www.snowsport.highland.com/sleddogs.htm** Tel: 01383 611 331 Scotland.

**www.saint-lary-guide.com/as_trainchien.htm** France

**http://fbdumoulin.free.fr/** Tel: 00 33 4 76 95 36 64 France

Husky Forever. Tel: 00 33 6 87 76 02 66 France

**www.kiska-vercors.com** Tel: 00 33 4 75 48 27 16 France.

**www.exodus.co.uk** Tel: 0870 240 5550 France.

**www.waldschrat-adventure.de** Tel: 00 49 9 926 1731 Germany.

**www.husky-saas-fee.ch** Tel: 00 41 79 589 5804 Switzerland.

**www.arctic-experience.co.uk** 01737 214 214

**www.adventuresportsholidays.com** 01273 872 242

**www.axehandle.nu** Tel: 00 46 644 700 06 Sweden.

**www.husky-holiday.com** Tel: 00 46 642 701 10

**www.emagine-travel.co.uk** tel 0870 902 5399 Finnish Lapland.

## Why is this good for families?

Younger children can ride inside as passengers (say from age three) while older children (say 13 and upwards) and adults can drive their own teams.

## Pros

• All the exhilaration of winter sports with almost no risk.

• Everybody loves dogs.

## Cons

• If the snow conditions are unsuitable (too deep, too soft) it'll be a chore rather than a joy.

## Where to go

Among the 'usual destinations' the French Alps and Pyrenees are good; among the less usual try Lapland.

## When

March for the combination of good snow, sunshine and daylight.

## Price guide

Unfortunately, running dog teams tends to be expensive. Expect to pay around £100 a day to drive your own team. For a two day trip staying in a refuge you'll pay around £225. Husky-Holiday charges £1,600 for what it calls the Minitarod, a two week version of the world's most famous dog race.

## More fun wintersports ideas for the whole family

Lots of resorts have ice-skating rinks, either indoors or out. If you'd like to try it beforehand there are 40 or so ice rinks in the UK, including four in London, and a couple each in Wales and Scotland. For general information take a look at **www.iceskating.org.uk** and **www.dotukdirectory.co.uk/Sport?Ice_Skating**.

Older children might take to curling, which is bowls on ice and played between two teams of four curlers (**www.englishcurling.co.uk**). The Royal Marine Hotel and Leisure Club in Brora, Sutherland has special weekend curling packages which cost £145 per person. See **www.highlandescapehotels.com/reservations/packages.asp** (Tel: 01408 621 252).

Most children love tobogganing. The latest style is the *airboard* (**www.airboard.com**), an inflatable luge, particularly popular at the French resort of Les Orres in the Hautes-Alpes (Tourist Office Tel: 00 33 4 92 44 01 61). You can also tow it behind a boat.

Ranch El Colorado at the French resorts of Arc 2000 and Arc 1950 (Tel: 00 33 4 7907 0605) has horses that will pull the kids along on their skis (an activity known as ski-joering in French). Lots of resorts, particularly the Austrian ones, also have sleigh rides.

---

## And finally

A group of friends wanted somewhere to stay high up in the mountains so they could get an early start for skiing and snowboarding. So they built an igloo. When more friends turned up they built another. Then another. They got rather good at it. Now they build whole villages and charge people. There are five different locations – Gstaad, Engelberg, Scuol, Zermatt and Zugspitze. Neither you nor the kids have to be tough. True, your bed is ice but it's covered in sheepskin and you each get an expedition quality sleeping bag as well. What's more, every igloo village has either a whirlpool or a sauna. Prices start at around £100 per person per night. **www.iglu-dorf.com** Tel: 00 41 416 122 728.

# Chapter 15

# Christmas And New Year Holidays

**Unusual family holidays in this chapter: looking for the real Father Christmas, the tallest Christmas Tree and the aurora borealis; Christmas Day on the beach; New Year's fireworks – and much more.**

Christmas is, of course, a time for families like no other. And it's understandable that lots of children relish Christmas at home. After all, how is Father Christmas going to find them if they're away? But, increasingly, families are taking holidays over the Christmas and New Year period. And instead of waiting for Father Christmas to come and find them they're going to look for him.

## Unusual Family Holiday No. 64: Looking For The *Real* Father Christmas

So where does the real Father Christmas actually live? Well, here are some theories.

1 **The North Pole, the Arctic**. We checked this one out. We can state categorically that no one answering to the name of Father Christmas or wearing a red suit does or ever has lived at the North Pole. Points: 0 out of 10.

2 **The North Pole, Wilmington, New York State**. Now this one is more convincing. For a start, there is actually a pole and it's covered in ice even in the summer. So that's a good start. There are also reindeer and a sleigh, kiddie rides, shows and, yes, a fat man in a red suit. Points: 6 out of 10. **www.roadsideamerica.com** Tel: 00 1 518 946 2211.

3 **Perrygrove Railway Station**. A railway station in the Royal Forest of Dean in Gloucestershire sounds an unlikely place to find the real Father Christmas. But this Father Christmas passes the test of

arriving down the chimney. Now that's impressive. Children get to see him by first of all taking a ride on the steam train to collect magic badges from Jack Frost. Back at the station they rub them to make Father Christmas appear. Points: 7 out of 10. **www. perrygrove.co.uk** Tel: 01594 834 991.

4 **Butlins**. Could it be that the man in the red coat actually is a Redcoat? Well, that's what Butlins claims. And they've got the Christmas Grotto to prove it. Not to mention pantomimes, fireworks and a five-course Christmas feast. But, hang on, they say Father Christmas is not only in Bognor Regis but Minehead and Skegness as well. Must have some very fast reindeer. Mmm. Suspicious. Points: 7 out of 10. **www.butlinsonline.co.uk** Tel: 0870 242 2002.

5 **Rovaniemi, Lapland**. The claim that Father Christmas comes from Lapland is one that has to be taken seriously and the Rovaniemi area, right on the Arctic Circle, certainly seems to be the kind of place you'd expect to find him. Apparently, he used to live at the mysterious village of Korvatunturi but wanted to be nearer an air- port. Now Santa Claus' Village is just 2km away from Rovaniemi airport and, apparently, the International Aviation Association recognises it as Santa's official runway, not so much for getting his reindeer airborne as bringing thousands of tourists to visit. So that's pretty convincing. Obviously you can meet Santa and at his post office arrange for him to send you Christmas greetings. There's snow from October to May, his reindeer of course, the magical blue light that's known as *kaamos* and, if you're lucky, the aurora bore- alis. In Rovaniemi (5mi/8km) there's a Santa Claus musical. The only problem is the huge number of visitors at Christmas time but you can get over that by going early – and thus giving Santa Claus plenty of time to make your presents. Points: 9 out of 10. **www. santaclausvillage.info/** Tel: 00 358 16 356 2096.

## FURTHER INFORMATION

### Some tour operators

**www.transun.co.uk** Tel: 0870 444 4747

**www.activitiesabroad.com** Tel: 01670 789 991

**www.santatrips.com** Tel: 0870 811 0018

**www.responsibletravel.com** Tel: 01273 600 030

## Some questions to ask

✓ Is this the real Father Christmas?

✓ Will we actually be able to meet him?

✓ Can we meet the elves?

✓ Can we pat the reindeer?

✓ Are there reindeer rides?

✓ Is thermal outer clothing included (in the case of Lapland)?

## Why is this good for families?

Ho, ho, ho! Very funny!

## Pros

- Your children will really believe in Father Christmas, now.

## Cons

- Do you really want teenagers who believe in Father Christmas?

## Where to go

In addition to the places we checked out (above) there are quite a few more claiming to have the real Father Christmas, including several theme parks that stay open year round or re-open for Christmas (see Chapter 11).

## When

The closer it is to Christmas the busier Father Christmas gets.

## Price guide

A four night stay at Butlins at Christmas costs from around £350 self-catering for two adults and two children. An all inclusive one day visit to Santa Claus' Village in Finnish Lapland can cost around £400 while a four day trip costs around £1,000 – entrance to the village itself is free.

### The Aurora Borealis

Also known as the Northern Lights, the aurora borealis is a breathtaking natural light show, often in the form of a greenish-blue or red arc in the Arctic night. It can last for several hours but as it retreats towards the pole so the shapes become increasingly changeable and dramatic until nothing is left except a diffuse white glow.

The aurora borealis is something everybody from lower latitudes should see at least once and Christmas is a pretty good time to try. The phenomenon isn't normally seen in lower latitudes because the electrons and protons arriving as part of the solar wind are drawn towards the magnetic poles. As they collide with oxygen and nitrogen atoms in the atmosphere so they leave excited ions which emit radiation and create the weird colours.

The farther north you can go the greater your chance. During a Christmas/New Year break Scotland is a possibility and the Shetland Islands are a better one. But to have a really good chance you need to get inside the Arctic Circle which means a trip to northern Scandinavia. Best of all is a Norwegian Coastal Voyage, well away from light pollution and with no mountains to intervene.

**www.fjordtravel.no** Tel: 00 47 55 13 13 10

**www.cruisingholidays.co.uk** Tel: 01756 670 6510

## Skiing At Christmas

Christmas and New Year are very expensive times on the slopes. But go the week *before* Christmas and you can expect to pay only half as much for your lift pass and accommodation (depending on the resort). If you like the idea, see the previous chapter.

## Unusual Family Holiday No. 65: Christmas On The Beach

You might feel that Christmas in the sunshine somehow just isn't *right*. But reflect that it's the way it's always been in the southern hemisphere. In Australia, Christmas means the beach not the Queen's Speech; the sand and surf not the sofa and the snooze. And very nice it can be, too. But you don't have to go down under to be pretty certain of Christmas sunshine.

### The Canary Islands

**Chance of Christmas on the beach: 9/10.** The Canaries may belong to Spain but geographically they're Africa. Only a short distance off the coast of southern Morocco they're almost on the Tropic of Cancer. There's considerable variation between the islands and even between the north and south of the same islands – there's about seven degrees Celsius difference between the north and south of Gran Canaria, for example. Given average luck the temperature is likely to be about 20 degrees C (68F) and if it's sunny, which it should be (the December average is about six hours a day on Gran Canaria) then it'll feel even warmer. As for swimming, the sea will be 19 degrees C (66F) which is only three degrees below the summer temperature.

**Christmas celebrations:** The Canaries' Christmas is Spanish style but with local variations. Try yam served with sugar or honey. Children don't leave mince pies for Father Christmas but water and straw for the camels belonging to the Three Kings. It's they who bring the gifts, usually arriving on boats on the night of January 5th (Epiphany). So if you want to experience all the season's celebrations you need to stay for two weeks.

**Other things to do:** Sunbathing, swimming, surfing, diving, riding a camel to Timanfaya National Park (Lanzarote), climbing to the top of El Teide (3,710m/12,160ft; Tenerife).

## Florida

**Chance of Christmas on the beach: 8/10.** Best bet is the southern part of Florida, especially the Florida Keys where there are just two inches of rain in December (5.1cm) and temperatures vary only between 21 degrees C (67F) and 24 degrees C (76F).

**Christmas celebrations:** It may be the 'Sunshine State' but there are Santas everywhere including the theme parks and even the trains (Tel: 00 1 877 869 0800). You'll even experience sub-zero temperatures in the 'Florida Fridge' at Gaylord Palms, Orlando – two million pounds of ice are sculpted into polar bears, castles, a nativity scene, Father Christmas's grotto and much more **www.gaylordpalms.com/ice** Tel: 00 1 407 586 4423. On 25th December 1837 soldiers built a fort 20 miles east of present day Orlando and called it Fort Christmas. Today there's a full size replica plus restored historical homes and people think it's fun to send their cards from the local post office, postmarked 'Christmas, Florida' **www.nbbd.com/godo/FortChristmas/**.

**Other things to do:** Sunbathing, swimming, diving, visiting Florida's theme parks.

## California

**Chance of Christmas on the beach: 7/10.** California is the third largest state extending for about 800 miles (1,300km) north to south. So don't make the mistake of going to the northern part. In fact, you might as well get as far south as you can, which is San Diego, just 30 minutes from the Mexican frontier. With only 1.36 inches of rain in December (3.44cm) San Diego has a 73 per cent chance of sunshine on Christmas Day. But you'll still be a lot farther north than either the Florida Keys or the Canary Islands.

**Christmas celebrations:** If you like sun and sand and you don't mind the traditional paraphernalia of Christmas being given a new twist then California's beaches are hard to beat. All along the coast you'll find Santas arriving on Harley Davidson bikes or even on surfboards.

**Other things to do:** San Diego has an early season Parade of Lights as well as a Balloon Parade. If you're staying further north there are California's famous theme parks (see Chapter 11). You could even go skiing - the resorts of the Lake Tahoe area, for example, are a mere 200 mile drive east of San Francisco.

## The Christmas Day/New Year's Day Plunge

There's nothing like a dip in cold water to shake off the holiday season lethargy. At Hungtinton Beach, California, on New Year's Day, they jump from the pier or fun run into the sea at 10am (Main Street) **www.beachcalifornia.com** while at Santa Monica beach you could join hundreds of others in what they call the Polar Bear Beach Plunge **www.resolutionfest.com** Tel: 00 1 310 474 6832.

If they think California water is cold they obviously have no idea where polar bears live. At Coney Island, New York, they also have a 'Polar Bear' Club and the temperature on New Year's Day is usually 33 degrees F – that's one degree above freezing. Now that's more like it. If you want to join the fun see **www.polarbearclub.org** Tel: 00 1 718 356 7741.

The inhabitants of Achill Island, County Mayo, one of the most westerly points in Europe, claim to be among the last Europeans to enjoy the sun on New Year's Eve. But, then, that also means they're the last to see the sun arrive on New Year's Day. Which makes their traditional dip in the Atlantic from the beach at Dugort all the bolder **www.achilltourism.com/newyear.html** Tel: 00 353 98 47 353.

Better still, join the 150 or so others at Rhu Marina at noon on New Year's Day who brave not only the waters of Loch Lomond but the monster as well **www.stayatlochlomond.com**.

But as everyone knows, the real place to find polar bears is Hampstead ponds. Mr Bear swims on Christmas morning and for some strange reason Mrs Bear swims on New Year's Day Tel: 020 8348 9908.

## Unusual Family Holiday No. 66: Hogmanay

Hogmanay, for anyone who doesn't know, is New Year's Eve in Scotland. And they really know how to throw a ceilidh. Which, for the benefit of Sassenachs (English people) is pronounced *kaylee* and means a party. The celebrations in Edinburgh last three days *at least* (**www.edinburghshogmanay.org**). They begin with a Torchlight Procession through the streets to watch the fireworks at Carlton Hill (usually on 29th December). The famous Night Afore is a riotous street party. Then comes the big night itself, attracting one hundred thousand people from all over the world. Fireworks are launched from Edinburgh Castle and six other sites around the city. To make it a really memorable night you need tickets for the Concert in the Gardens and for the Ceilidh in the Assembly Rooms.

Four other great places to celebrate New Year are:

**Berlin**. The firework display at the Brandenburg Gate attracts a million revellers (Tel: 00 49 30 25 00 25).

**Cap de Creus**. It's the easternmost point in Spain. Party wherever you like then turn up at dawn to see the sun rise up out of the Mediterranean and drink hot chocolate.

**Reykjavik**. Christmas lights everywhere, lots of private fireworks parties (like Britain 50 years ago) and, starting just before midnight, one of Europe's biggest fireworks displays.

**Trafalgar Square**. This one's hard to beat. You get the Christmas Tree from Norway, a good old sing song and a New Year's Day dip in the fountains all in one place.

### And finally

If you want to recreate the sort of Christmas you see on Christmas cards and boxes of chocolates get along to the ice-skating rink at Kew Gardens. Right in front of the giant conservatory known as the Temperate House it's an enchanting experience for all the family. £10 adults/£7.50 children **www.kewgardensicerink.com** Tel: 0870 400 0797.

## And even more finally

If you've each got a Santa Claus outfit (suit, hat and beard) you can get free entry to Europa-Park (see Chapter 11) on the first day of the Christmas season (usually around the beginning of December). In 2006 there were 10,128 Santas, all enjoying the rides and attractions, which set a record for the park **www.europa-park.de** Tel: 00 49 0 18 05 77 66 88.

## Useful contacts

You'll find all the websites referred to in this book on our website at **www.whiteladderpress.com** to make it easier for you to access them. Click on 'Useful contacts' next to the information about this book.

### Contact us

You're welcome to contact White Ladder Press if you have any questions or comments for either us or the author. Please use whichever of the following routes suits you.

**Phone** 01803 813343 between 9am and 5.30pm

**Email** enquiries@whiteladderpress.com

**Fax** 01803 813928

**Address** White Ladder Press, Great Ambrook, Near Ipplepen, Devon TQ12 5UL

**Website** www.whiteladderpress.com

## What can our website do for you?

If you want more information about any of our books, you'll find it at **www.whiteladderpress.com**. In particular you'll find extracts from each of our books, and reviews of those that are already published. We also run special offers on future titles if you order online before publication. And you can request a copy of our free catalogue.

Many of our books also have links pages, useful addresses and so on relevant to the subject of the book. You'll also find out a bit more about us and, if you're a writer yourself, you'll find our submission guidelines for authors. So please check us out and let us know if you have any comments, questions or suggestions.

# Ditch the Donkey

## Unusual holidays in the usual destinations

Fancy something a bit different for this year's holiday, but don't know what?

Maybe you're getting a little bored and jaded with the same old beach-based holiday every year. On the other hand, you just aren't intrepid enough to risk life and limb in extreme places to get your kicks. Then this book is for you.

What you need are ideas for exciting holidays without going too far from your usual destinations. Did you know you could rent a cabin cruiser in Venice? Go on pilgrimage to Santiago de Compostela? Learn to tango in Miami? Or enjoy a wine-tasting holiday in France? There are thousands of holidays out there just waiting for you to go and enjoy them.

Here, at last, is all the inspiration you need. Every page is stuffed with ideas to fire your enthusiasm for:

- castaway, hideaway and romantic breaks
- sport, extreme sport, adventure and snow holidays
- family breaks and holidays with animals
- holidays with the locals, educational and working holidays
- cultural and mind, body, spirit holidays

Travel journalists Paul Jenner and Christine Smith give you all the contact details, website addresses, price guidelines, pros and cons, and other practical information you could need to persuade you to ditch the donkey and try something a bit different next time.

"Out-of-the-ordinary holidays are now easy to find; this is the travel guidebook that dares to be different."
**Desmond Balmer (editor THE GOOD HOTEL GUIDE)**                    **£9.99**

# Au Revoir Angleterre

## MAKING A GO OF MOVING ABROAD

### Paul Jenner & Christine Smith

"Realistic, extremely helpful and easy to read; a nice mixture of common sense and encouragement. Bravo! The book covers every basic question that a potential expatriate could reasonably ask." **Peter Mayle**

"Humorous, true to life and terribly entertaining. For anyone thinking of leaving the country this is a must have book."
**John Burton Race**

**So life in Britain is getting you down. The rain, the bills, the daily grind. There's got to be something better, surely?**

Suppose you lived abroad. Maybe Spain? Or perhaps the south of France? Or what about Greece? Portugal? Croatia? You'd certainly enjoy a better climate. And you'd be able to try a different way of life. It would be less stressful, healthier, cheaper, and better for the kids. You could even learn to water ski, or convert an old building, or own your own olive grove. Heaven!

Then again, you could find your problems travel with you. You miss your family and friends, you don't speak the language well enough and you can't make head nor tail of all the form filling you have to do in order to buy your dream home.

Paul Jenner and Christine Smith, expats who have lived in several countries overseas, have researched the most popular reasons Brits have for wanting to live abroad. In this book they will guide you through the pitfalls and highlights, the pros and cons of each one, so you know just what you're doing, and never regret saying 'Au Revoir Angleterre'.

*"Au Revoir Angleterre* **is a funny and practical look at the dream and reality of moving abroad. If everybody read it there would be no TV programmes about naive expats and their ruined dreams. Essential reading."** *Rosemary Bailey author of* **Life In A Postcard – Escape to the French Pyrenees.**

**"Don't move a muscle till you've taken the Jenner and Smith reality check ..."** *Christopher Somerville travel writer and columnist*

£9.99

# Tidy Your Room

## Getting your kids to do the things they hate

Are you sick of yelling at the kids to hang up their clothes? Tired of telling them to do their homework? Fed up nagging them to put their plate in the dishwasher? You're not the only one. Here, at last, is a practical guide to help you motivate them and get them on your side.

Parenting journalist Jane Bidder draws on the advice of many other parents as well as her own experience as a mother of three, to bring you this invaluable guide to getting your kids to do the things they hate.

The book includes:
- what chores are suitable at what age, and how to get them to co-operate
- getting homework done without stress
- where pocket money fits into the equation

**Tidy Your Room** is the book for any parent with a child from toddlerhood through to leaving home, and anyone who has ever had trouble getting their kids to do chores or homework. That's just about all of us, then.

Jane Bidder is a professional author and journalist who writes extensively for parents. She also writes fiction as Sophie King. She has three children, the eldest two of whom are now at university, so she has extensive personal as well as professional experience of getting kids to do the things they hate. She is the author of *What Every Parent Should Know Before Their Child Goes to University*.

Price £7.99

# KIDS&Co

"Ros Jay has had a brilliant idea, and what is more she has executed it brilliantly. **KIDS & CO** is the essential handbook for any manager about to commit the act of parenthood, and a thoroughly entertaining read for everyone else" **JOHN CLEESE**

**WHEN IT COMES TO RAISING YOUR KIDS, YOU KNOW MORE THAN YOU THINK.**

So you spent five or ten years working before you started your family? Maybe more? Well, don't waste those hard-learned skills. Use them on your kids. Treat your children like customers, like employees, like colleagues.

No, really.

Just because you're a parent, your business skills don't have to go out of the window when you walk in through the front door. You may sometimes feel that the kids get the better of you every time, but here's one weapon you have that they don't: all those business skills you already have and they know nothing about. Closing the sale, win/win negotiating, motivational skills and all the rest.

Ros Jay is a professsional author who writes on both business and parenting topics, in this case simultaneously. She is the mother of three young children and stepmother to another three grown-up ones.

**£6.99**

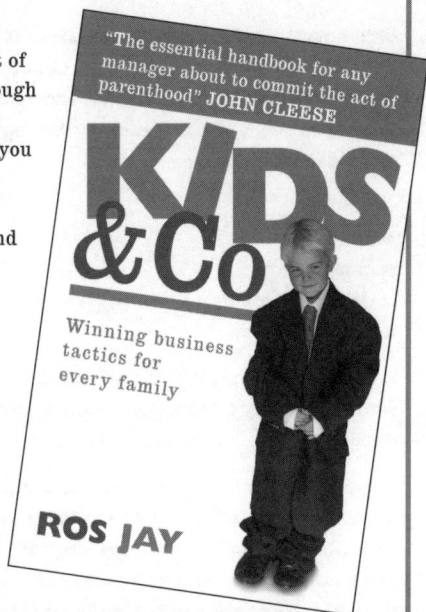

"The essential handbook for any manager about to commit the act of parenthood" JOHN CLEESE

KIDS & Co

Winning business tactics for every family

ROS JAY

# HOW TEENAGERS THINK

## an insider's guide to living with a teenager

## jellyellie

So you've got a teenager? I'm so sorry. Still, they were really cute once, and they'll grow up to be a credit to you. It's just these few years in between you have to get through. It's not so much the lack of conversation, or even the fact that they never open the curtains. It's the fact that most of the time you haven't a clue where they're coming from. They could be an alien species.

Until now. At last, a real live teenager is prepared to communicate (yes, actually communicate) about what makes teenagers tick. Fifteen year old jellyellie dishes the dirt on what she and the many fellow teenagers she interviews really think. Essential reading for all parents, she explains what teenagers think about:

● school
● friends
● money
● designer clothes
● sex and drugs

…and all the other things that feature strongly in teenage life. She tells you what encourages teenagers to co-operate with their parents and what pushes all their rebellious buttons.

jellyellie hit the headlines two years ago when she launched her hugely successful website all about bluejacking (don't ask).
Described by the *Guardian* as 'the voice of the msn generation' she's back to tell parents how to get the best possible relationship with their teenager without simply giving them everything they ask for.

£7.99

# Order form

You can order any of our books via any of the contact routes on page 108, including on our website. Or fill out the order form below and fax it or post it to us.

We'll normally send your copy out by first class post within 24 hours (but please allow five days for delivery). We don't charge postage and packing within the UK. Please add £1 per book for postage outside the UK.

Title (Mr/Mrs/Miss/Ms/Dr/Lord etc)

Name

Address

Postcode

Daytime phone number

Email

| No. of copies | Title | Price | Total £ |
|---|---|---|---|
|  |  |  |  |
|  |  |  |  |
|  |  |  |  |
|  |  |  |  |
|  |  |  |  |
|  | Postage and packing £1 per book (outside the UK only): |  |  |
|  | TOTAL: |  |  |

Please either send us a cheque made out to White Ladder Press Ltd or fill in the credit card details below.

Type of card  ☐ Visa  ☐ Mastercard  ☐ Switch

Card number

Start date (if on card) _____  Expiry date _____  Issue no (Switch) _____

Security code (last 3 digits on reverse of card) _____

Name as shown on card

Signature